Baritone Bass Clef Book 1

PREMIER PERFORMANCE

AN INNOVATIVE AND COMPREHENSIVE BAND METHOD

by Ed Sueta

Dear Band Student:

*Welcome to **Premier Performance**! Congratulations on your decision to learn to play the baritone. Learning to play the baritone will be a rewarding and satisfying experience. You will develop an appreciation for music which will be a source of enjoyment throughout your life.*

*By playing in the band, you will make new friends and have a great deal of fun performing for your family, classmates and community. Your band director, a good instrument, a desire to learn and **Premier Performance** will be all you need to begin your journey into the exciting world of instrumental music. With regular practice, you will quickly develop the musical skills necessary to become an outstanding musician.*

Best wishes for musical success!

Ed Sueta

Instruments provided courtesy
of **The Selmer Company, Inc.**

Special thanks to Fine Arts Supervisor **Richard Haas** and the students and teachers of the **Bloomfield Public Schools** for their participation in the photographs on pages 2 and 3.

PUTTING YOUR BARITONE TOGETHER

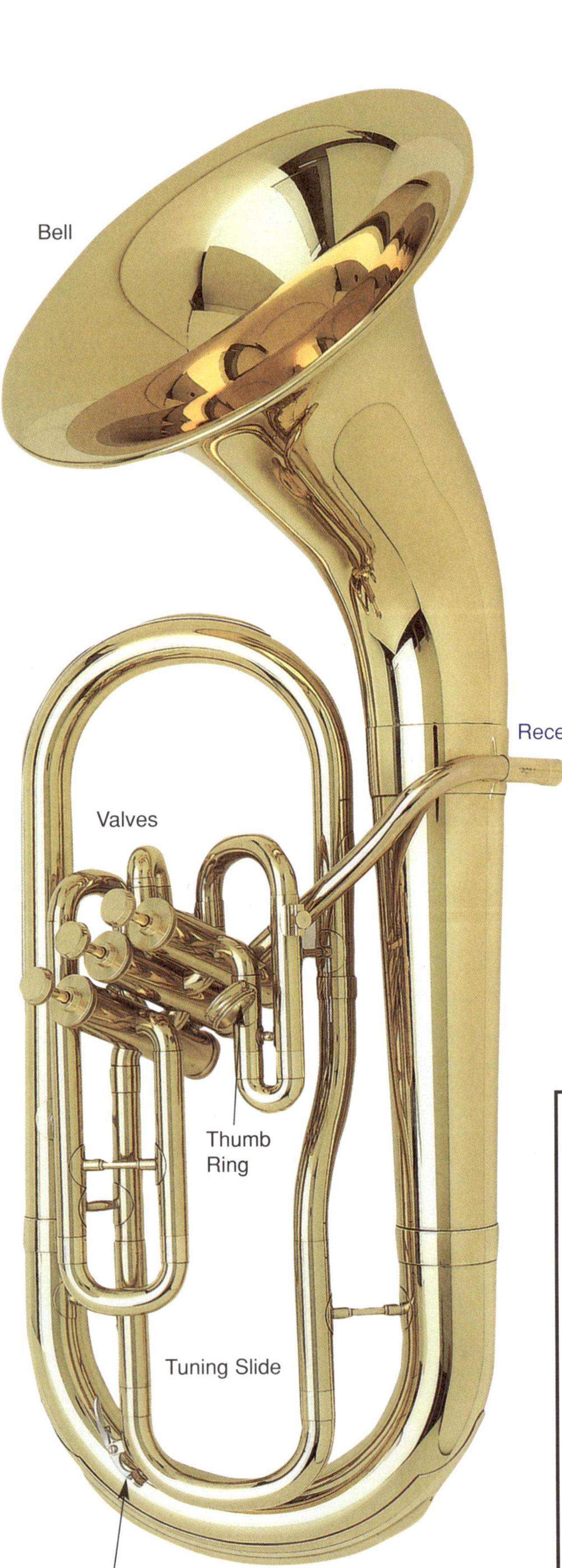

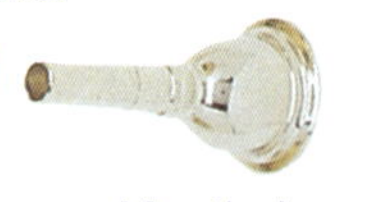

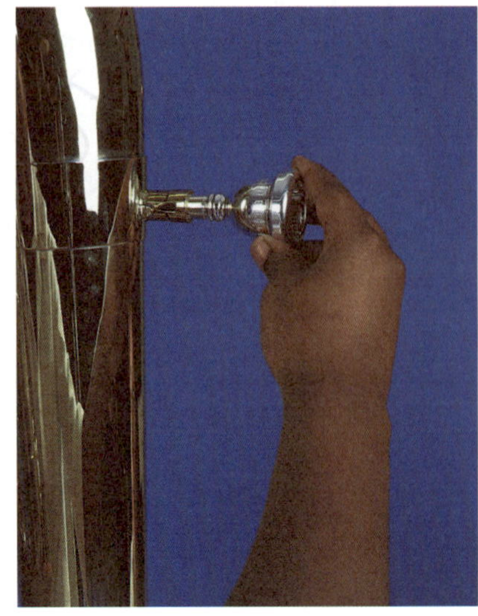

STEP ONE

◆ Take the mouthpiece in your right hand and gently insert it into the mouthpiece receiver. Gently twist the mouthpiece to the right.

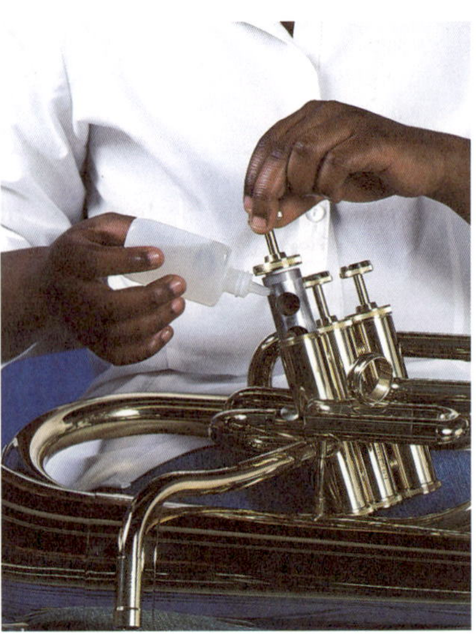

STEP TWO

◆ Unscrew the first valve cap by gently twisting it to the left. Do not unscrew the valve stem.
◆ Gently pull the valve part of the way out of the casing.
◆ Apply a few drops of oil to the valve.
◆ Slide the valve back into the casing making sure that the valve guide slides into the groove.
◆ Never force the valve if it will not move freely back into the casing.
◆ Tighten the valve cap by twisting it to the right.
◆ Repeat the steps listed above for the remaining valves.
◆ Pull the tuning slide out approximately $\frac{1}{4}$ of an inch.

BARITONE CARE

◆ When you are finished playing, depress the water key and blow through your instrument to remove any moisture.
◆ Wipe off your instrument with a soft, clean cloth.
◆ Remove your mouthpiece by gently twisting it to the left. Place the mouthpiece and your instrument in its case and latch it.
◆ Remember to grease all slides regularly. Make sure that any excess slide grease is removed with a clean cloth.
◆ Wash your mouthpiece with warm water on a regular basis. You may wish to use a special mouthpiece brush.

ALTERNATE METHOD FOR OILING VALVES

◆ Press down the first valve and pull the first valve slide straight out. Place several drops of valve oil into the tube. Keep the valve depressed as you replace the slide. Move the valve up and down several times.
◆ Repeat the above procedure with the other valves.
◆ Pull the tuning slide out approximately $\frac{1}{4}$ of an inch.

POSTURE AND PLAYING POSITION

◆ Sit up straight on the front part of your chair.
◆ Keep your head up, feet flat on the floor and look straight ahead.
◆ Relax your shoulders and move them down and back a little.
◆ Cradle your instrument in your lap.
◆ Reach around the left side of the instrument with your left hand and hold onto the tubing.
◆ Place your right thumb in the the thumb ring next to the valves.
◆ Your fingers should be slightly curved and touching the valve buttons.
◆ Keep your wrists straight and your elbows slightly away from your body.

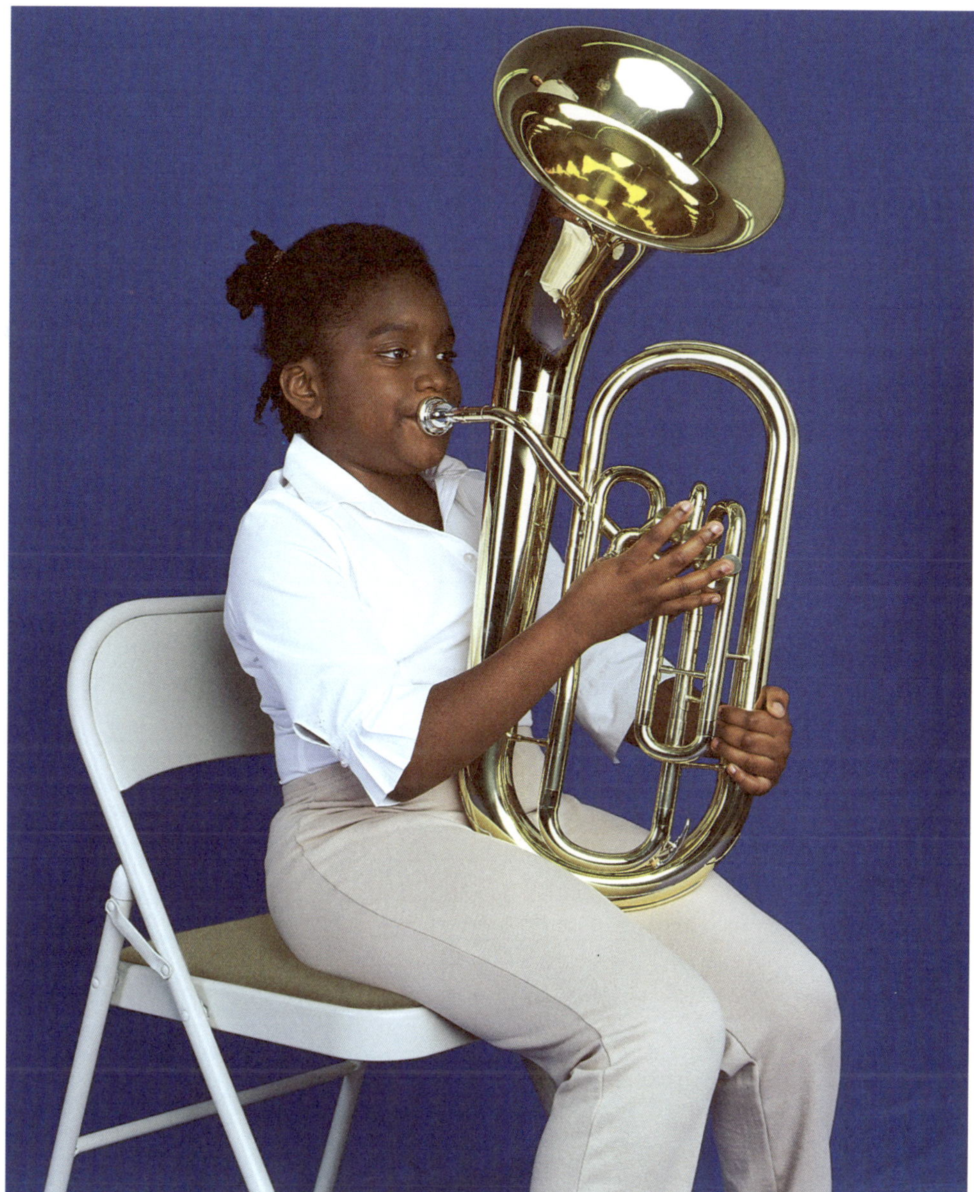

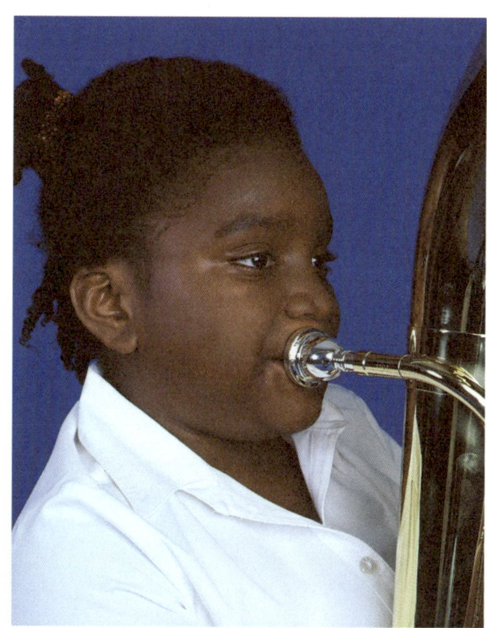

EMBOUCHURE

Producing a beautiful tone is one of your main goals when playing the baritone. The French word embouchure (ahm′ buh sure) describes the formation of your lips and mouth. Your embouchure and the air you breathe into the baritone will determine the quality of your tone.

◆ Place your lower teeth directly under your upper teeth with a slight separation between them.
◆ Place the mouthpiece on the center of your lips with ⅔ of the mouthpiece on your upper lip.
◆ Keep the corners of your lips firm to your teeth.
◆ Drop your jaw slightly and form your lips in an "em" position. You are ready to play your first tone.

PLAYING YOUR FIRST TONE

◆ Moisten your lips. Form your embouchure.
◆ Take a deep breath through the corners of your mouth. Keep your shoulders steady.
◆ Bring your lips firmly together and release your breath by whipering a firm "Too" which will create a buzzed tone. Make sure you keep your lips firm to the corners of your mouth.
◆ Hold the tone for several seconds.
◆ Always take deep breaths and use a firm air stream. Make your lip opening as small as possible.
◆ Repeat these steps several times.

Michael

PREMIER PROGRESS PRACTICE CHART

DATE	ASSIGNMENT/FOCUS POINTS	M	T	W	T	F	S	S	TOTAL	PARENT SIGNATURE
9/17		10	20	10			20	10	70	[signature]
9/24		15	20	marimba lab			5	35	75	[signature]
10/9	EXCELLENT TODAY - PAGE 11			X						
10/16	Pg 12 #17-22	15	30	10	30	10	10	15	120	[signature]
10/22	pg 13 #23 26	10	30	10	30	15	5	20	120	[signature]
10/24	pg 14 #30-32 (A, B+C)	10	30	15	30		10		90	[signature]
10/30	pg 15 #36 pg 16	X	30	X	30		5	10	85	[signature]
11/6	pg 17 9th up to #13		30		30	15	15		85	[signature]
11/15	pg 18 #48		30		30	20		10	80	[signature]

QUARTERLY GRADE ______

DATE	ASSIGNMENT/FOCUS POINTS	M	T	W	T	F	S	S	TOTAL	PARENT SIGNATURE
11/29	pg 18 #49		30							
12/6	BEETHOVEN - FIRST CONCERT		30		30					
12/18	pg 44 #1, 2		30							
1/28	pg 18 #47, 48, 51, 52		30		30					[signature]
2/5/08	pg 19 #55		30		30					[signature]
2/12/08	pg 20 #58		40		30					[signature]

QUARTERLY GRADE ______

DATE	ASSIGNMENT/FOCUS POINTS	M	T	W	T	F	S	S	TOTAL	PARENT SIGNATURE
3/6	pg 22 #64		30		30					
3/13	YANKEE SPIRIT		30		30					

QUARTERLY GRADE ______

DATE	ASSIGNMENT/FOCUS POINTS	M	T	W	T	F	S	S	TOTAL	PARENT SIGNATURE

QUARTERLY GRADE ______

FINAL GRADE ______

READING MUSIC

Music Staff

The music staff consists of 5 lines and 4 spaces.

Bass Clef

A bass clef sign is placed at the beginning of a music staff and indicates the position of the F. The F is on the fourth line of the staff.

Bar Line

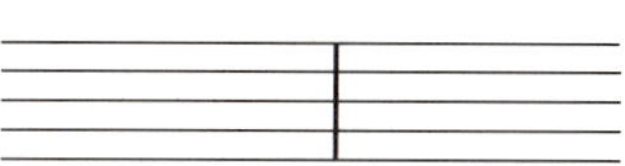

A bar line is a vertical line which divides the staff into measures.

Measure

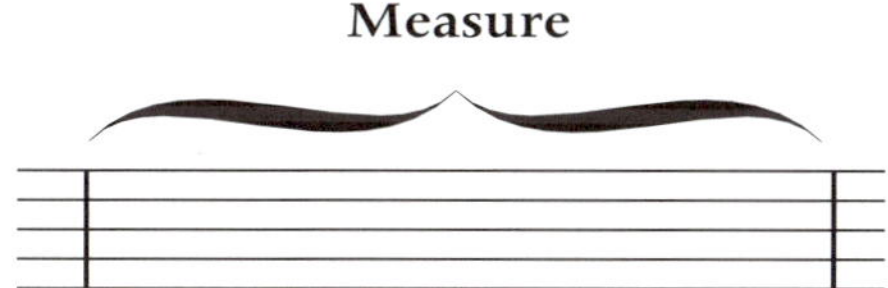

A measure is the distance between two bar lines.

Double Bar

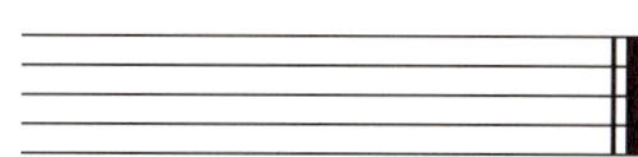

A double bar line marks the end of the music.

TIME SIGNATURES

4/4 = 4 beats in a measure = quarter note receives 1 beat

3/4 = 3 beats in a measure = quarter note receives 1 beat

2/4 = 2 beats in a measure = quarter note receives 1 beat

Whole note **Whole rest**

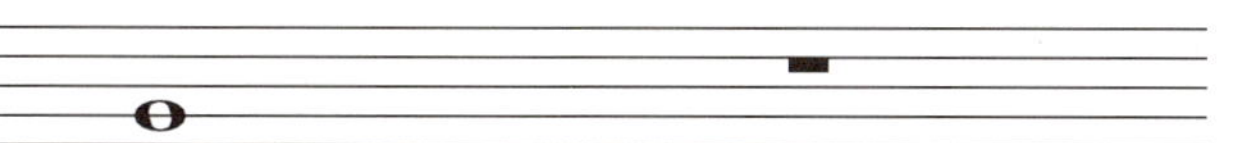

A whole note and whole rest each receive 4 beats in 4/4 time.

Half note **Half rest**

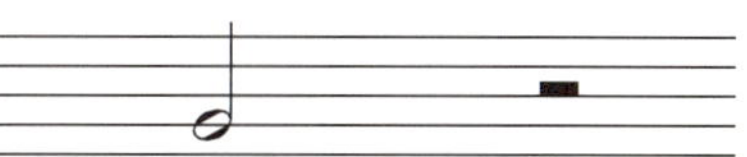

A half note and half rest each receive 2 beats in 4/4 time.

Quarter note **Quarter rest**

A quarter note and quarter rest each receive 1 beat in 4/4 time.

NAMES OF NOTES

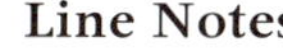

Line Notes

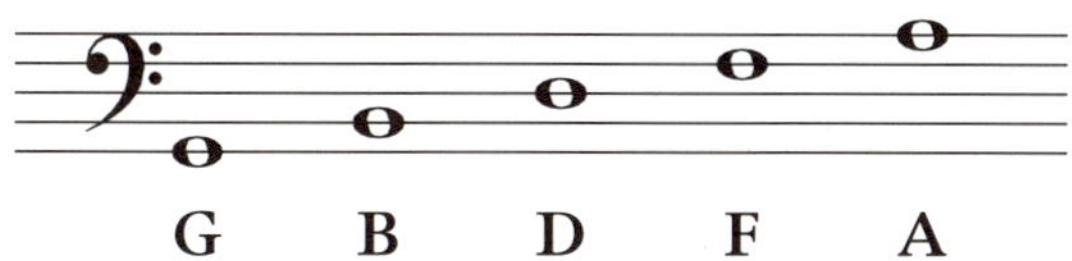

G B D F A

Memorize this sentence to remember the line notes: Girls (and) Boys Do Fine Always.

Space Notes

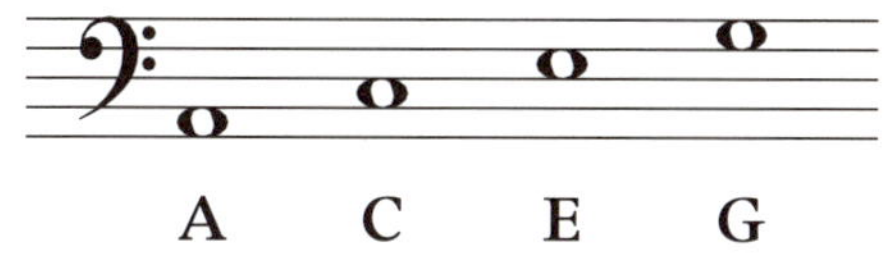

A C E G

Memorize this sentence to remember the space notes: All Cows Eat Grass.

E F G A B C D E F G A B C

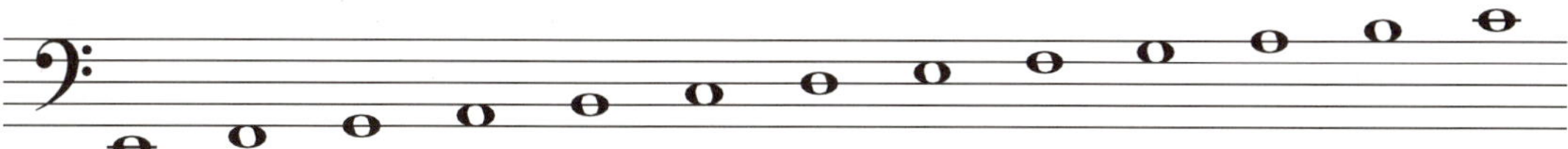

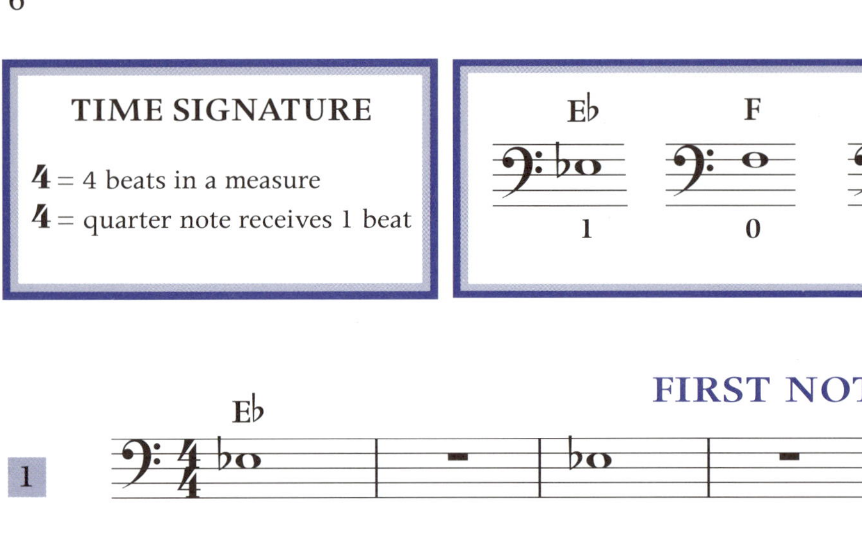

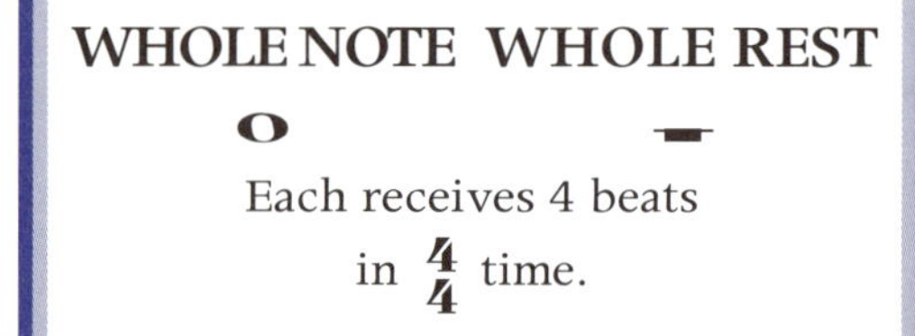

FIRST NOTE

1 E♭

A double bar marks the end of the music.

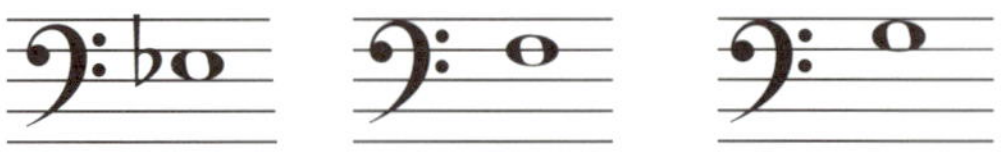

SECOND NOTE

2 F

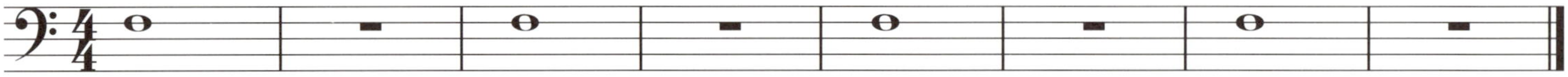

E♭ AND F

3

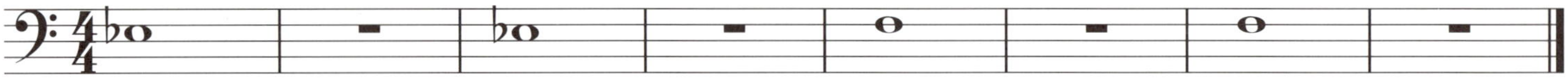

F AND E♭

4

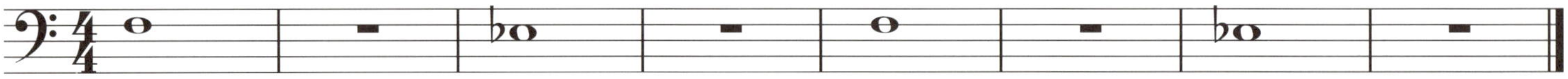

THIRD NOTE

5 G

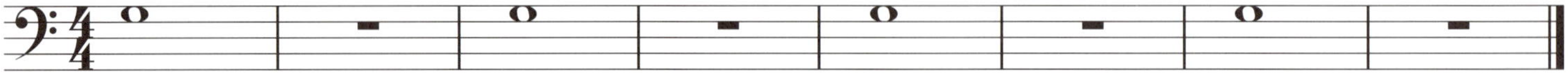

ALL THREE NOTES

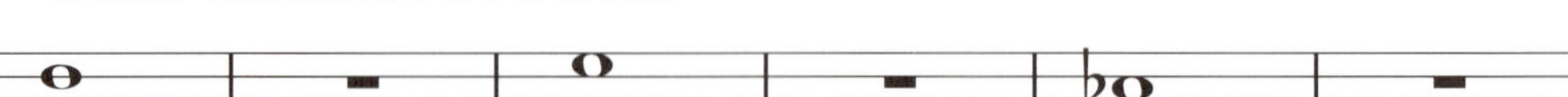

6

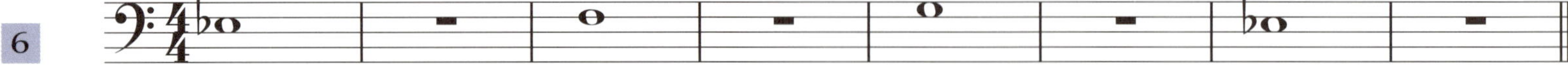

Move your fingers to the next note during the rests.

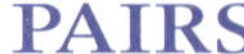

PAIRS

7

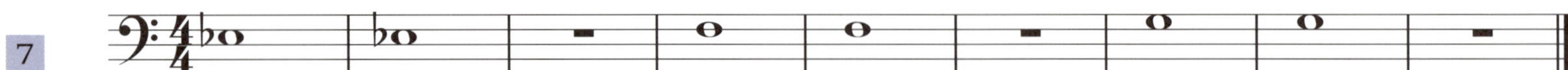

Read 2 notes.

UP AND DOWN

8

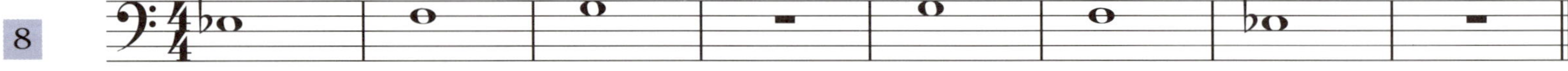

While playing one note, look ahead to the next note.

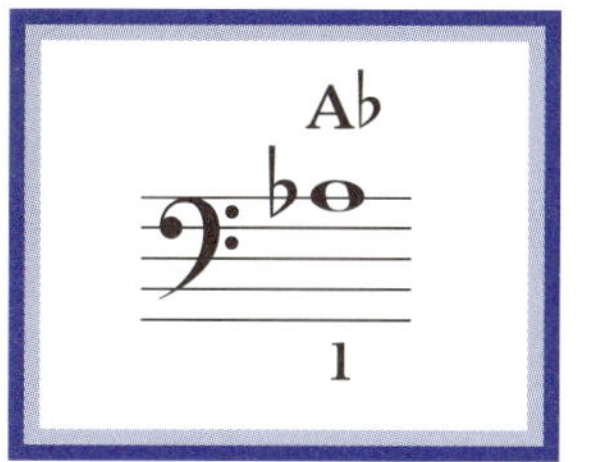

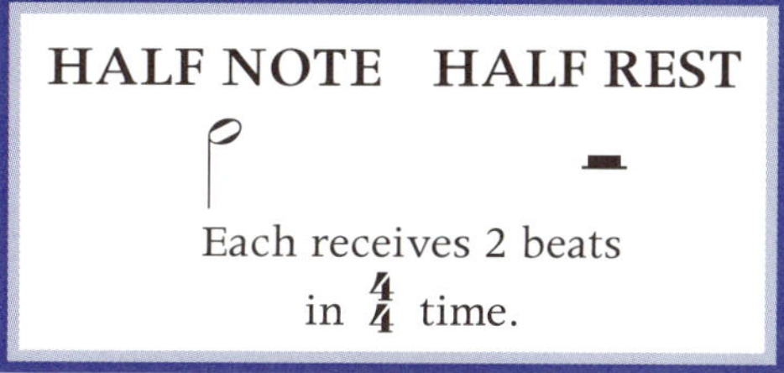

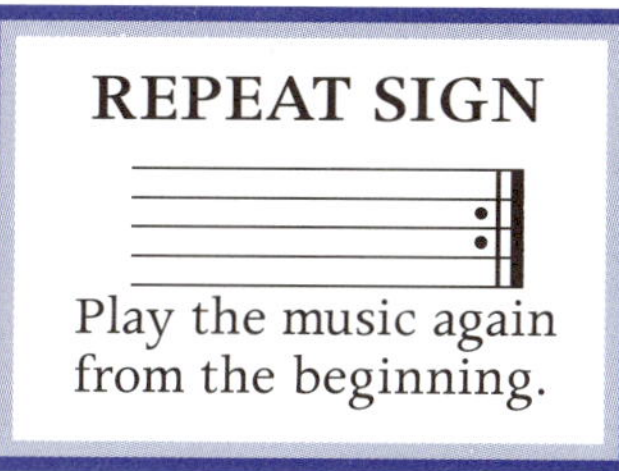

ALL A♭'S

9

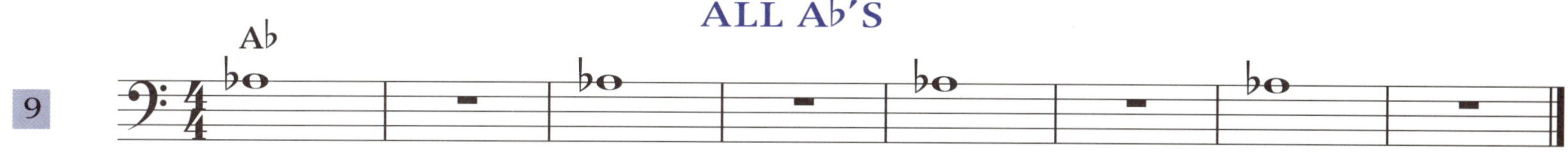

A♭ AND G

10

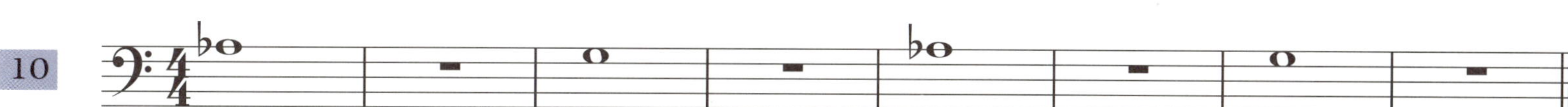

Always use your tongue (Too) to start each note.

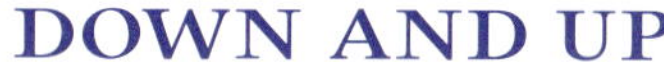

DOWN AND UP

11

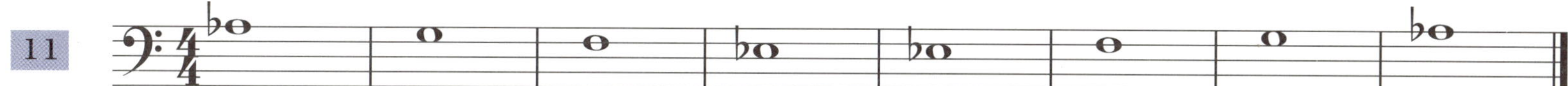

HALF NOTES - HALF RESTS

12

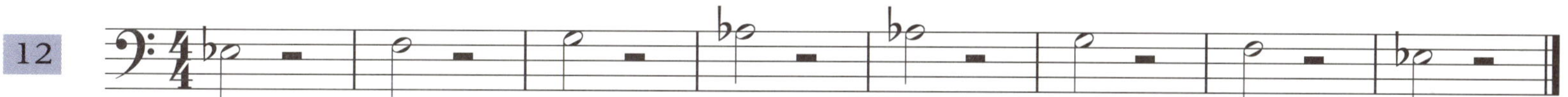

THE OTHER WAY

13

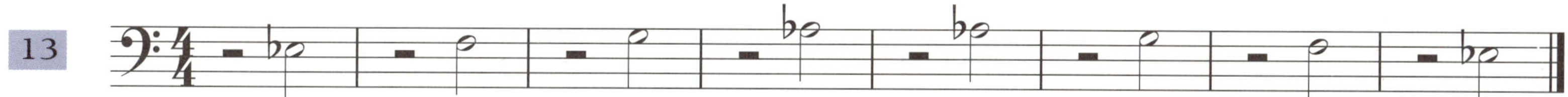

HALF AND WHOLE NOTES

14

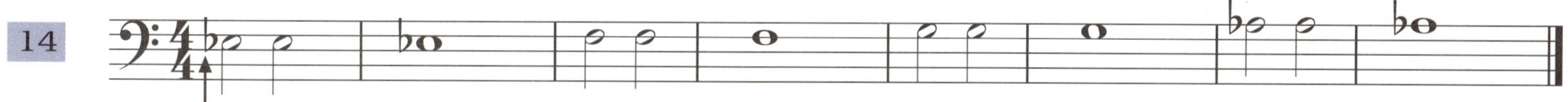

The first flat in the measure is for both notes in the measure.

A PARIS

French Tune

15

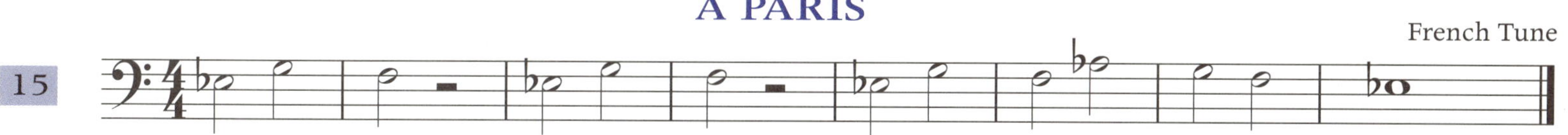

REPEATING

16

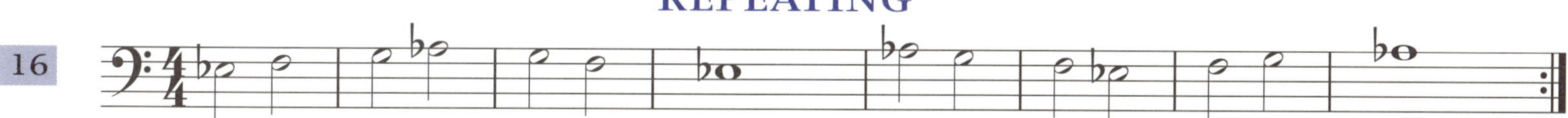

1. Play Line 16 several times. 2. Play as smoothly as you can.
3. Keep your fingers close to the tops of the valves.

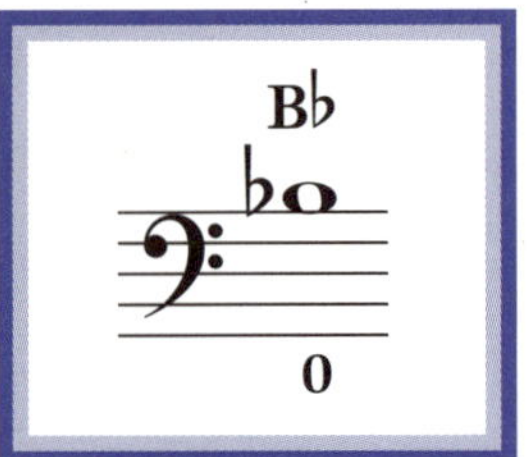

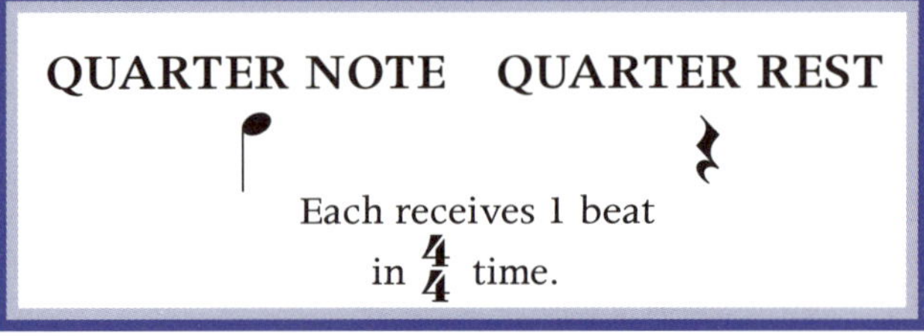

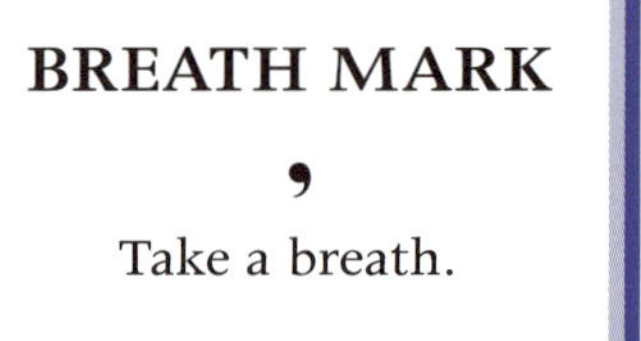

QUARTER NOTES

17

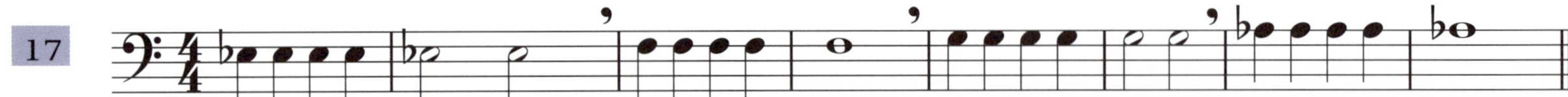

QUARTER RESTS

18

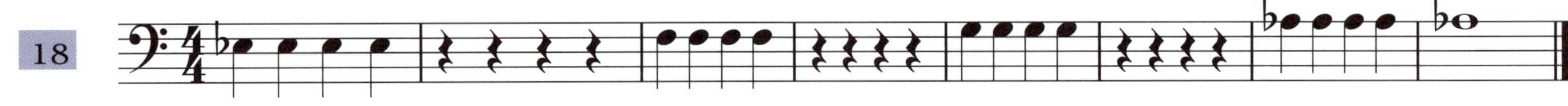

Tongue each quarter note clearly.

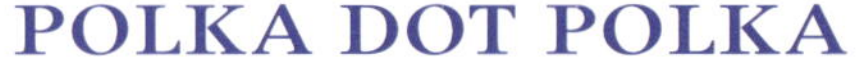

Ed Sueta

19

ALL B♭'S

20

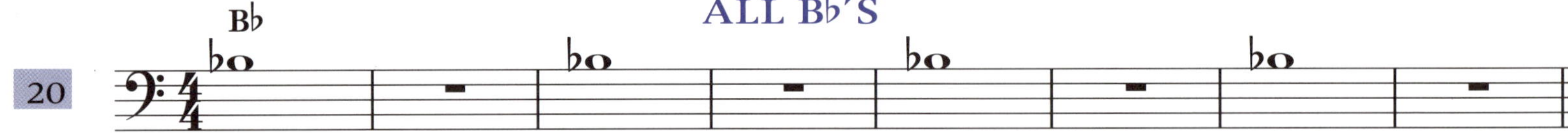

AIR CONTROL

Write in seconds

21

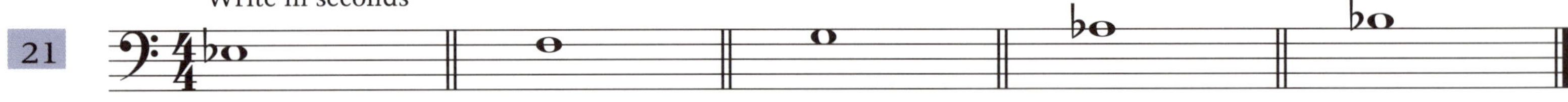

How many seconds can you hold each note?

FOR GOOD POSTURE

1. Sit straight 2. Head level 3. Shoulders down and back a little

SOME FOLKS DO

Stephen Foster (1826-1864)

22A

22B

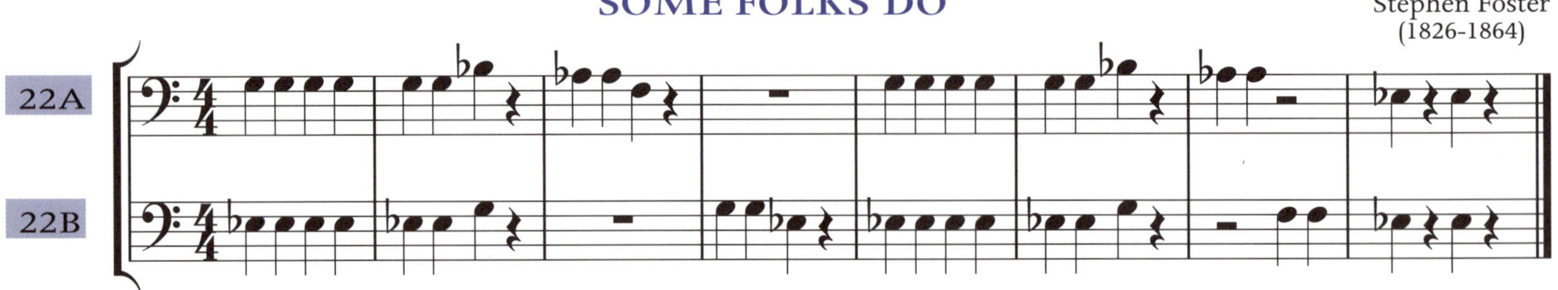

FIVE NOTE CHALLENGE

23

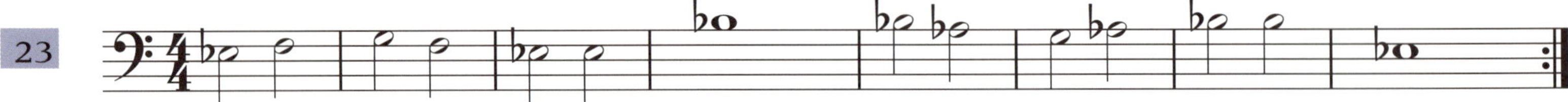

1. Play Line 23 several times. 2. When this challenge becomes easy, increase your speed.

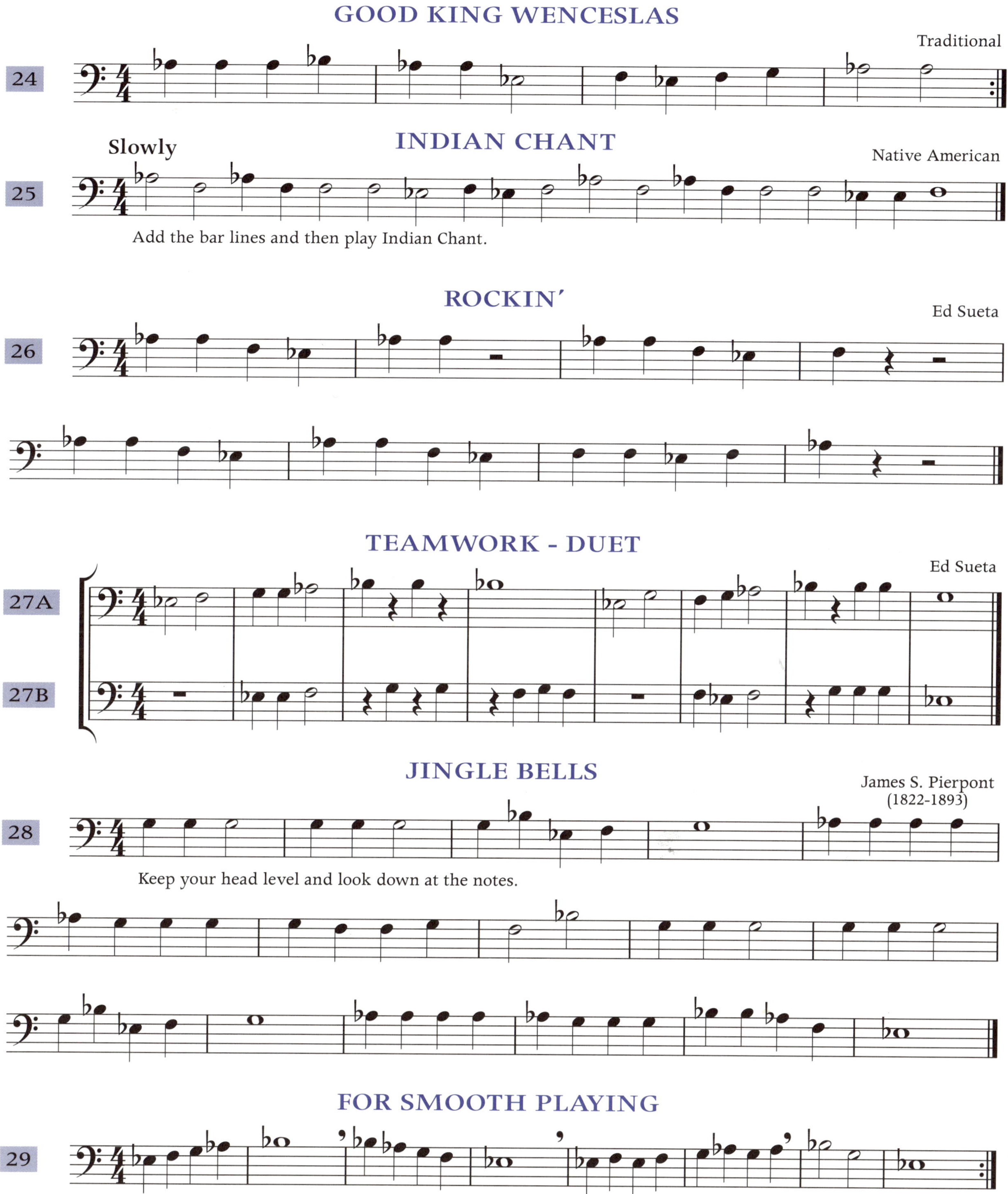
GOOD KING WENCESLAS
Traditional
24
Slowly
INDIAN CHANT
Native American
25
Add the bar lines and then play Indian Chant.
ROCKIN'
Ed Sueta
26
TEAMWORK - DUET
Ed Sueta
27A
27B
JINGLE BELLS
James S. Pierpont
(1822-1893)
28
Keep your head level and look down at the notes.
FOR SMOOTH PLAYING
29
Finger and say the notes before you play this line. Be sure to tongue each note clearly.

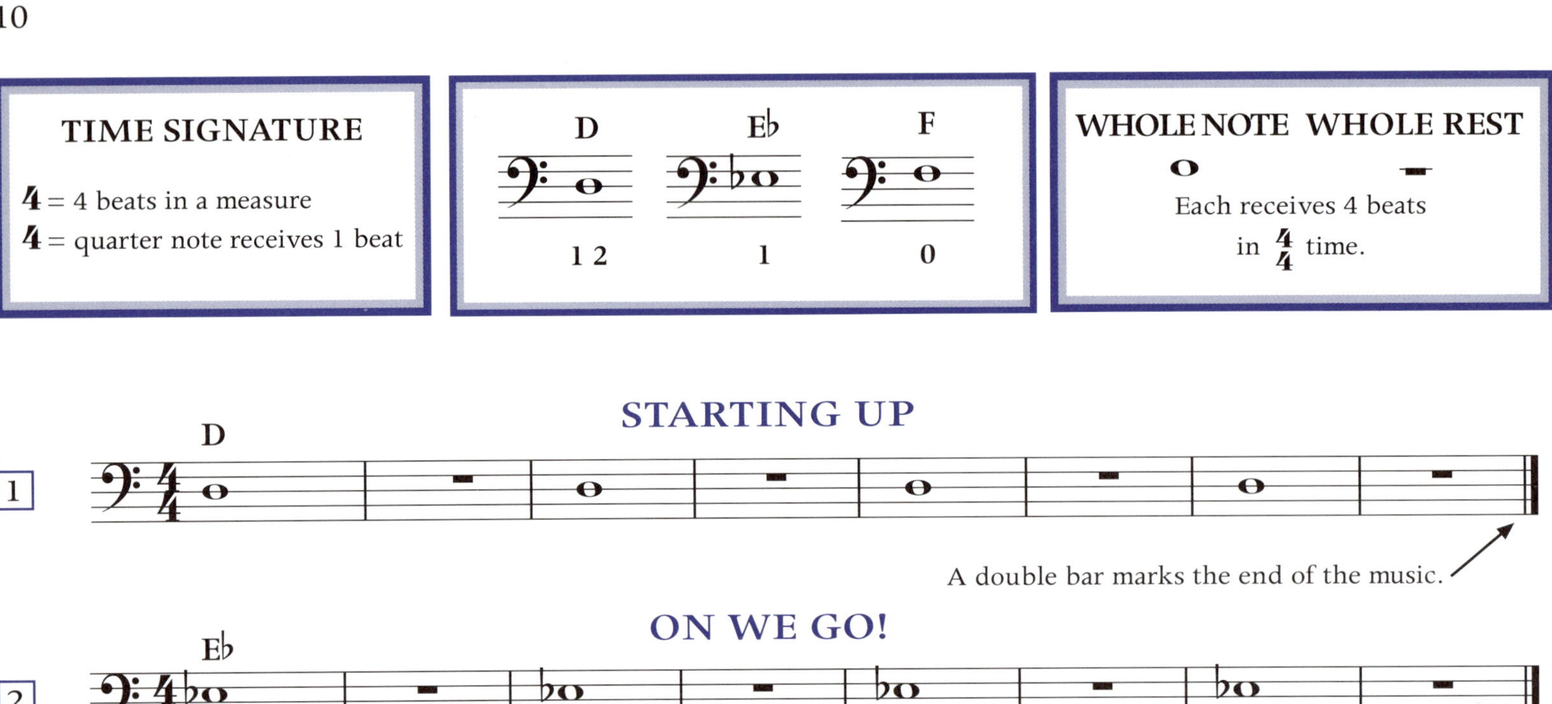

STARTING UP

1

ON WE GO!

2

KEEP IT SMOOTH

3

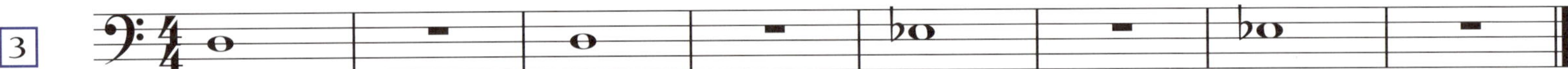

Always use your tongue (Too) to start each note.

DON'T HURRY

4

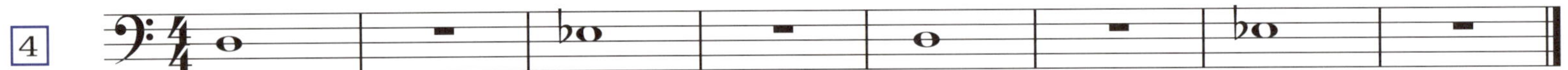

SOUNDING GOOD

5 F

KEEP IT STEADY

6

Move your fingers to the next note during the rests.

CONNECTIONS

7

While playing one note, look ahead to the next note.

LOOK AHEAD!

8

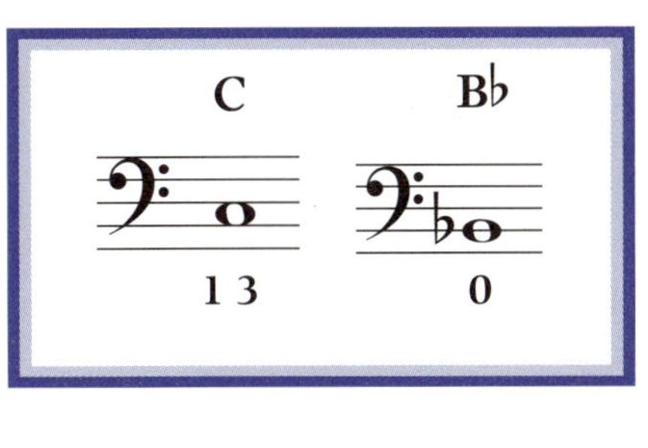

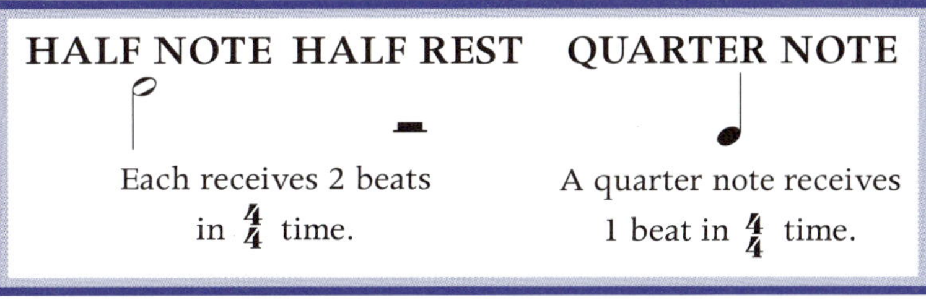

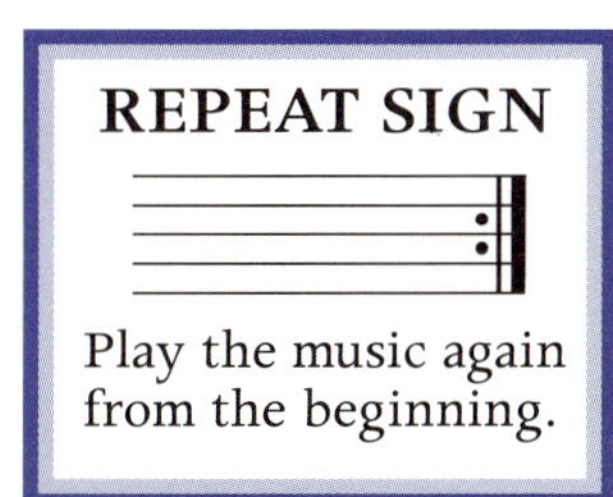

COUNT IT RIGHT

9

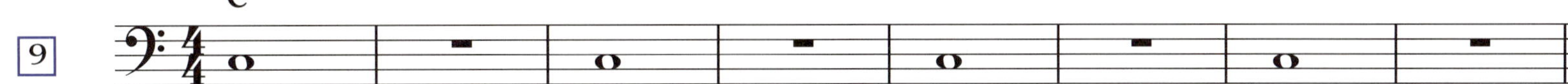

ACCURACY COUNTS

10

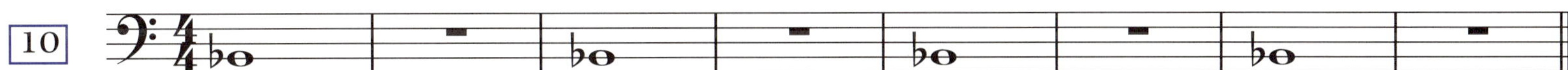

LISTEN!

11

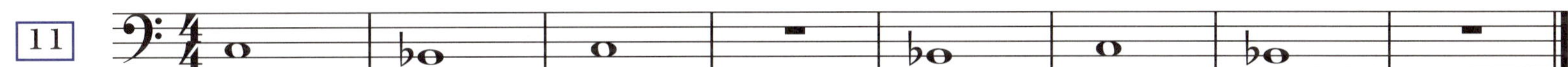

HALF NOTES ARE EASY!

12

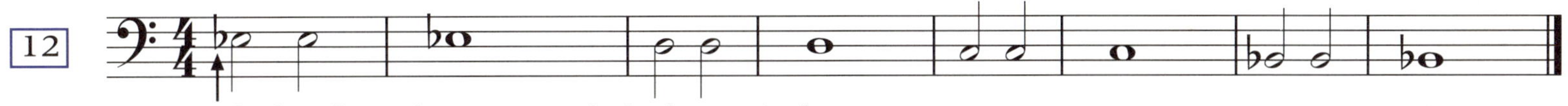

The first flat in the measure is for both notes in the measure.

HALF RESTS ARE EASY TOO!

13

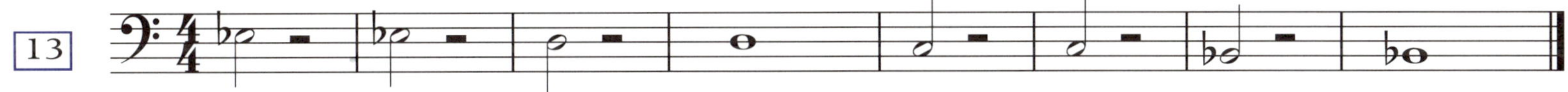

HALF RESTS THE OTHER WAY

14

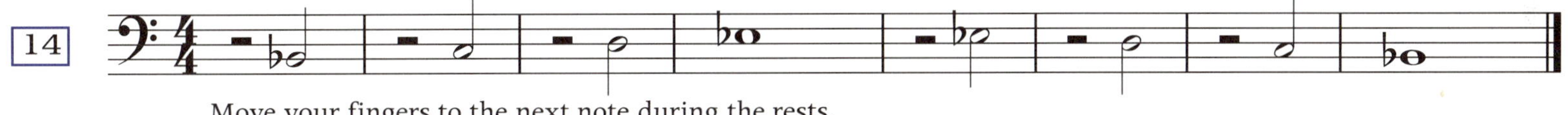

Move your fingers to the next note during the rests.

TIME TO REPEAT

15

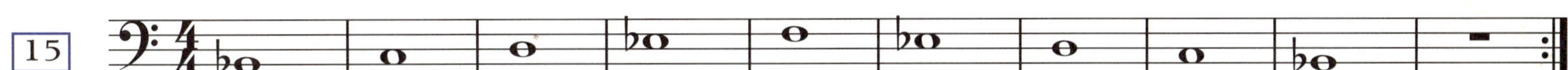

QUARTER NOTES

16

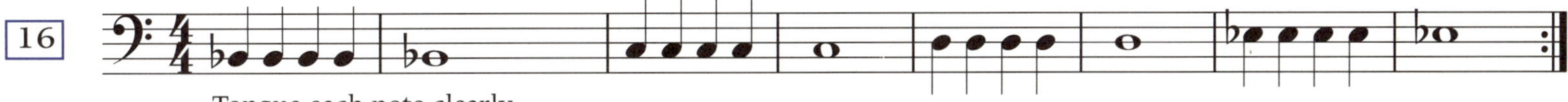

Tongue each note clearly.

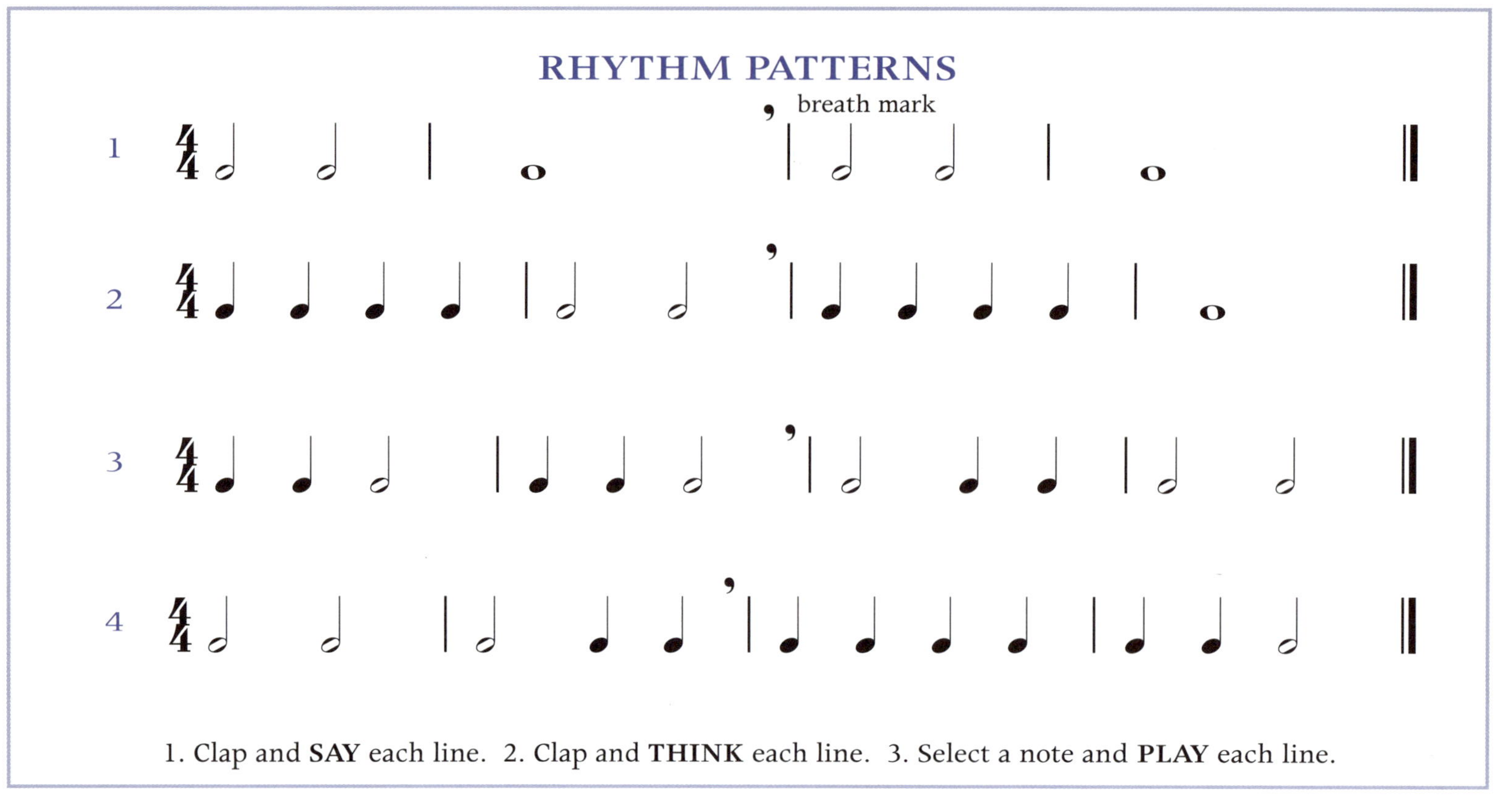

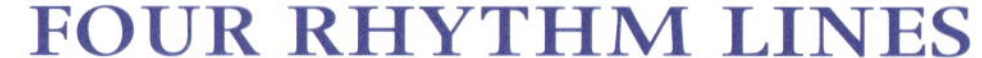

FOUR RHYTHM LINES

17

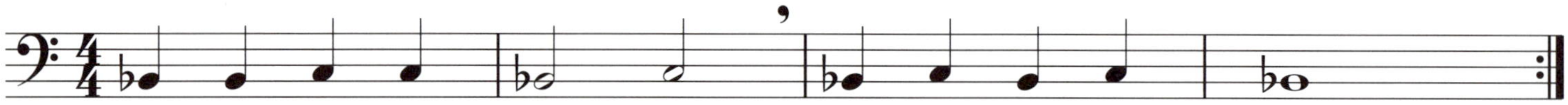

18

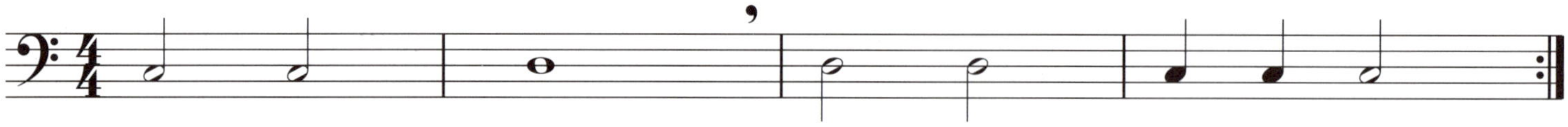

19

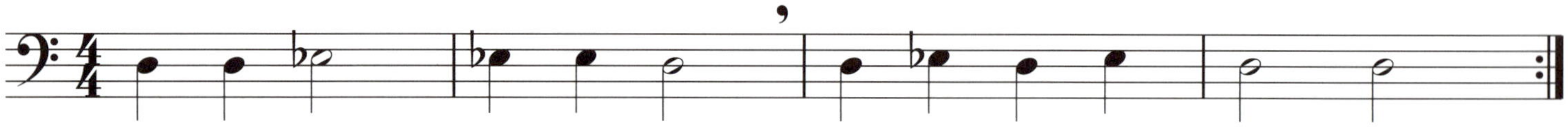

20

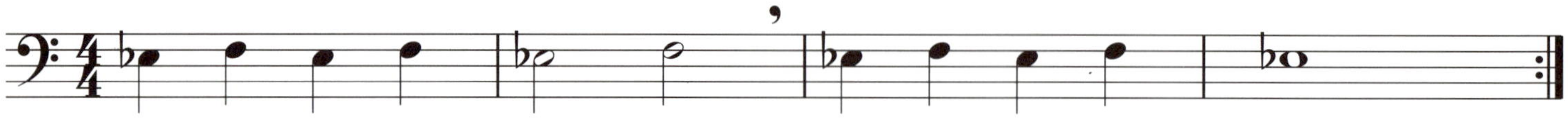

FRENCH SONG

Traditional

21

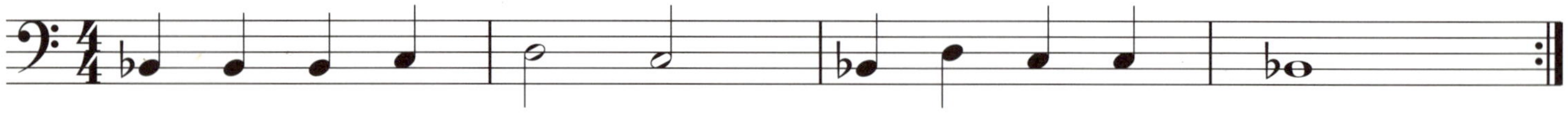

FOR SMOOTH PLAYING

22

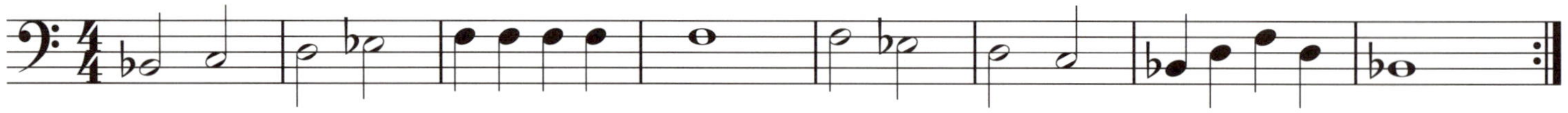

Finger and say each note before you play this line.

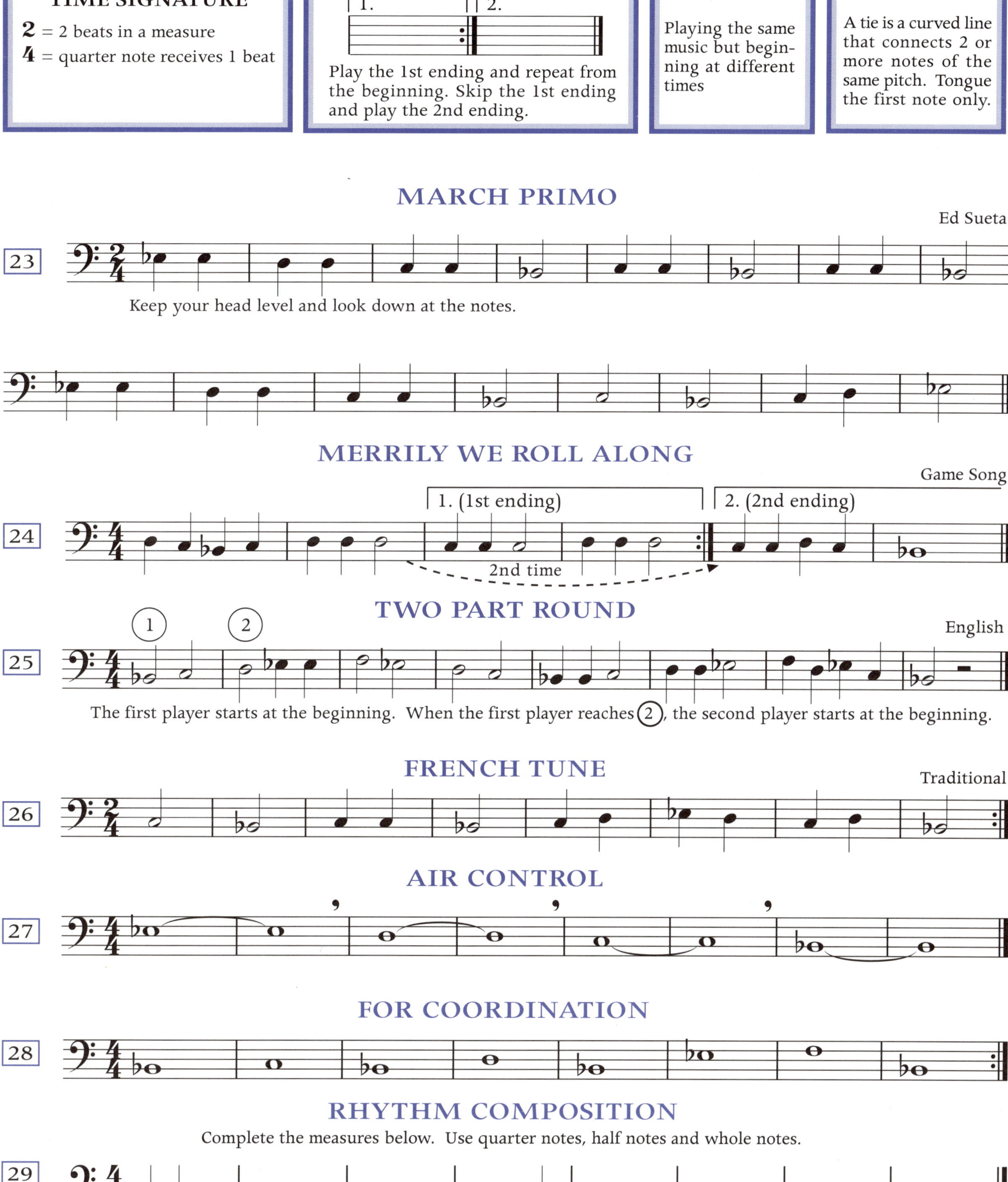

Play Premier Technique Lines 1 and 2 on page 44.

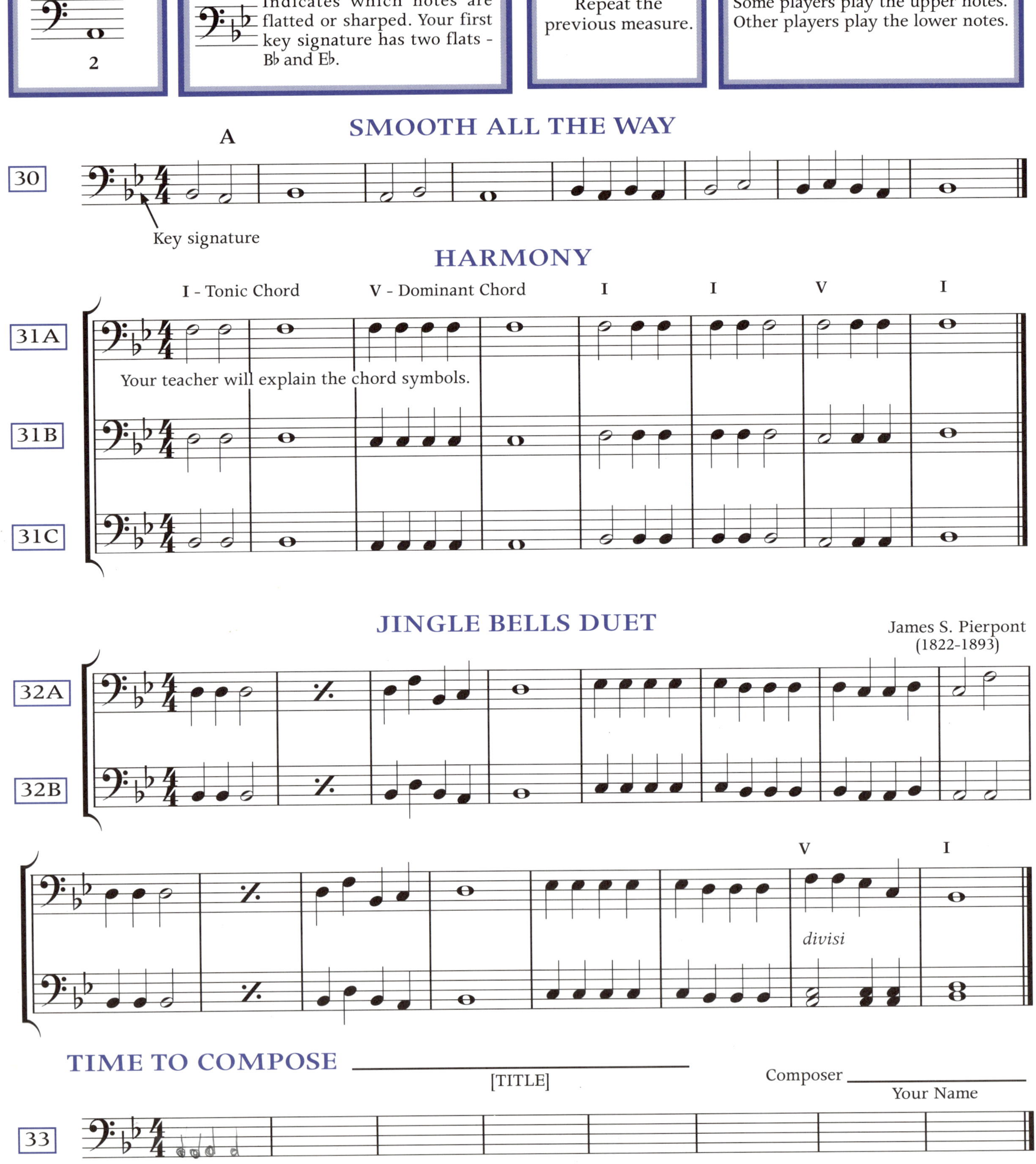

Use the Rhythm Composition you created in Line 29 and add notes to compose your own melody.
1. Start and end on B♭. 2. Use only the notes that you have learned. 3. Name your composition. 4. Play your composition.

Play Premier Technique Lines 3 and 4 on page 44.

G

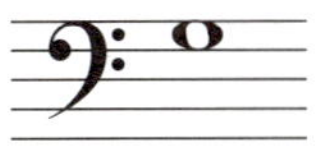

1 2

QUARTER REST

A quarter rest receives 1 beat in 2/4, 3/4 and 4/4 time.

SOLO
One person plays

UNISON
All players play the same notes

ACCENT

>

Play more air.

STEADY DOES IT

34

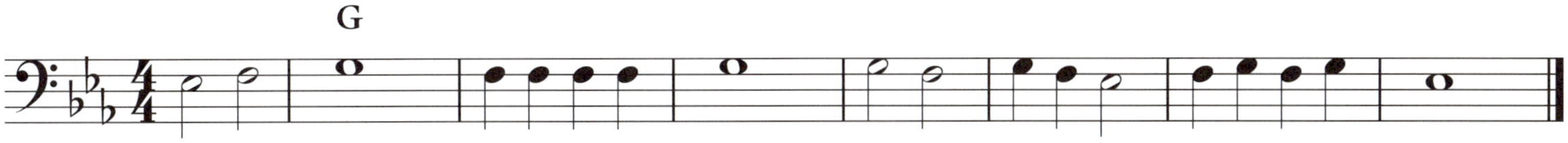

G

QUALITY CONTROL

35

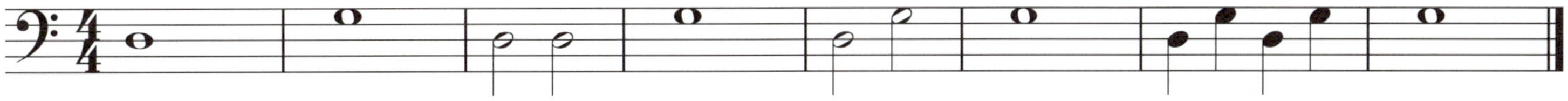

JOLLY OLD ST. NICK

Traditional

36A

36B

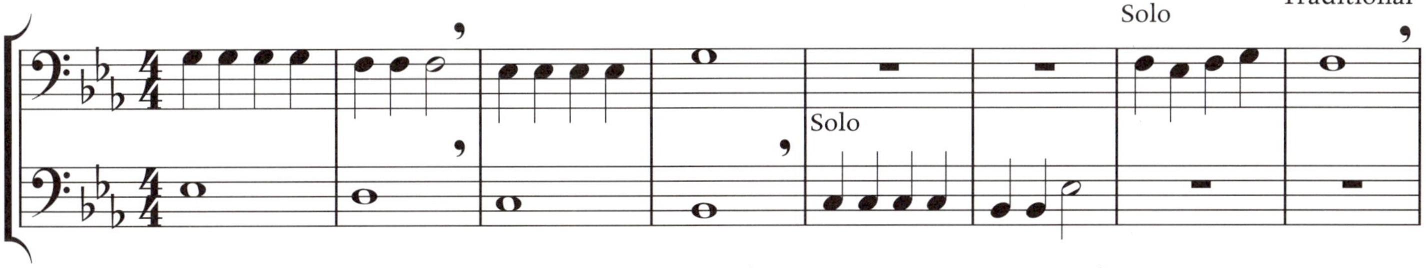

Solo

Solo

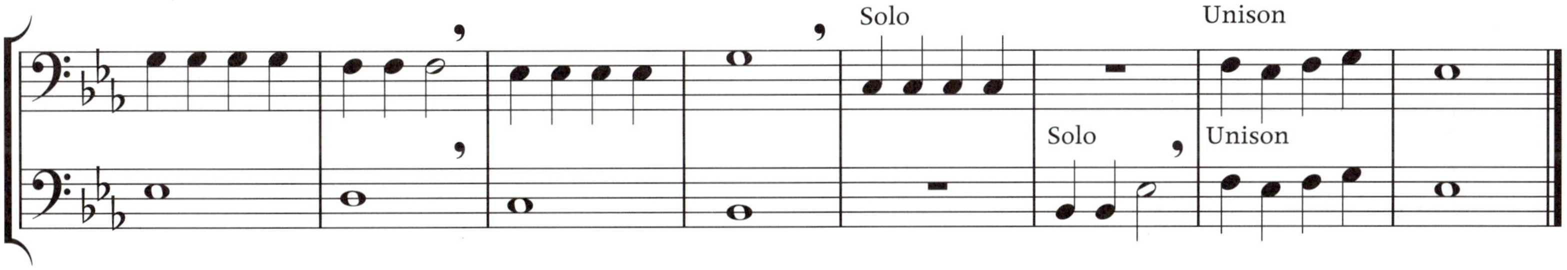

Solo

Unison

Solo

Unison

POLKA DOT POLKA

Ed Sueta

37

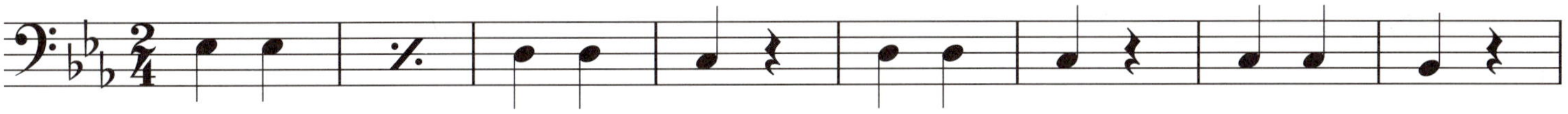

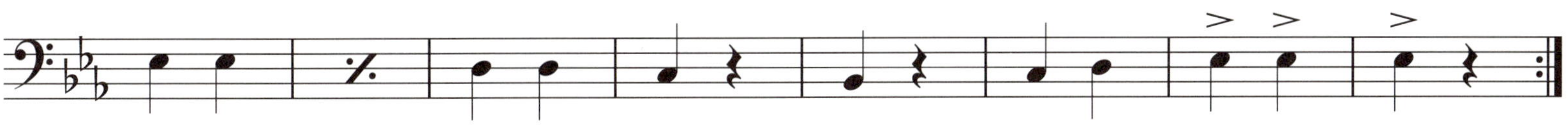

FOR SMOOTH TECHNIQUE

38 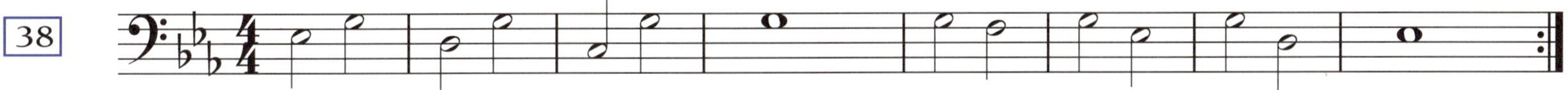

Play Premier Rhythm Lines 1, 2 and 3 on page 42.

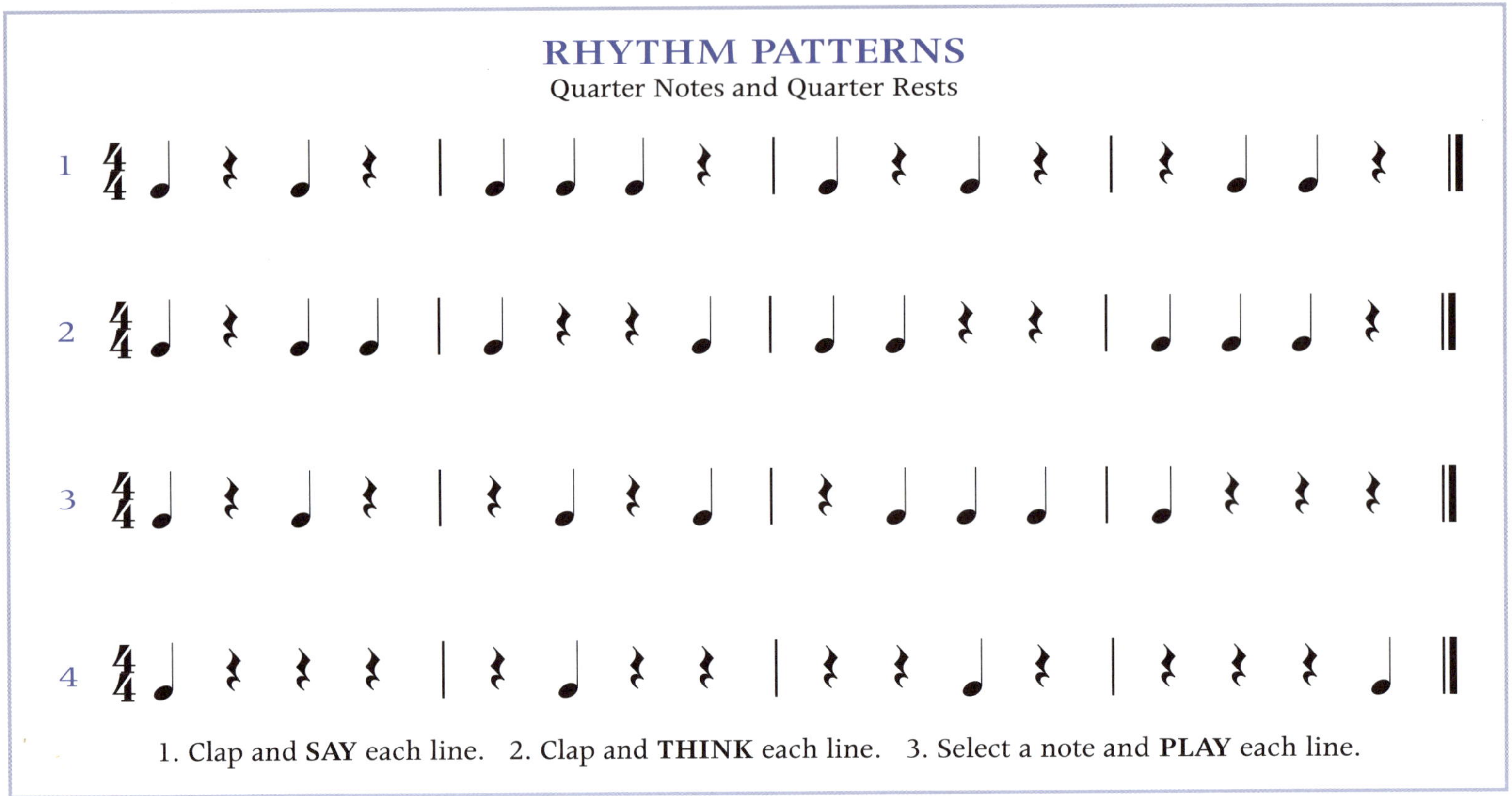

REST TEST

39

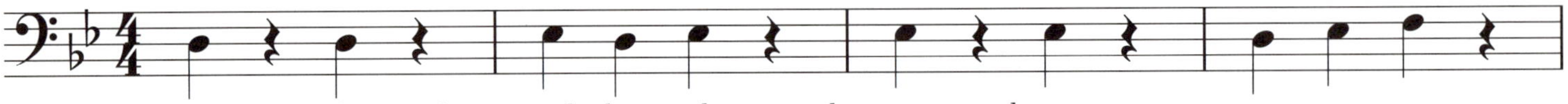

To keep your place in the music, look at each note and rest as you play.

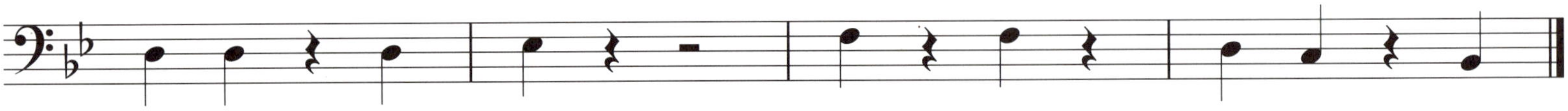

DUO DE ESPAÑA

SPANISH DUET

Ed Sueta

40A

40B

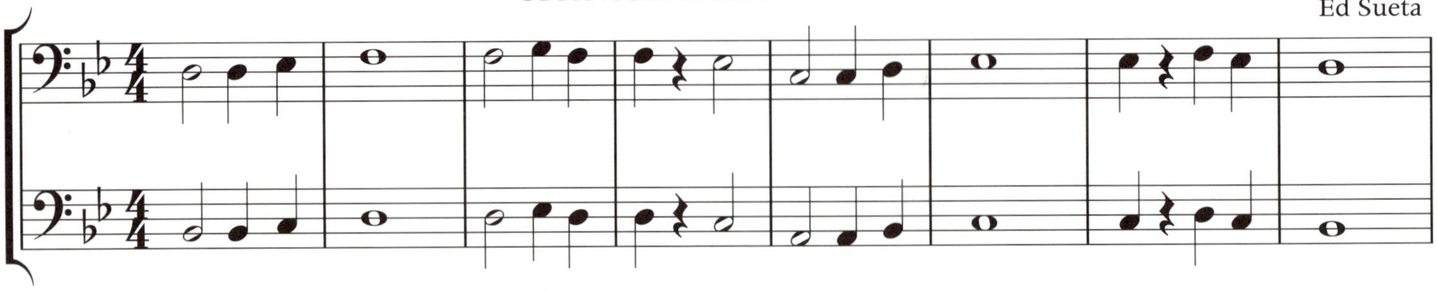

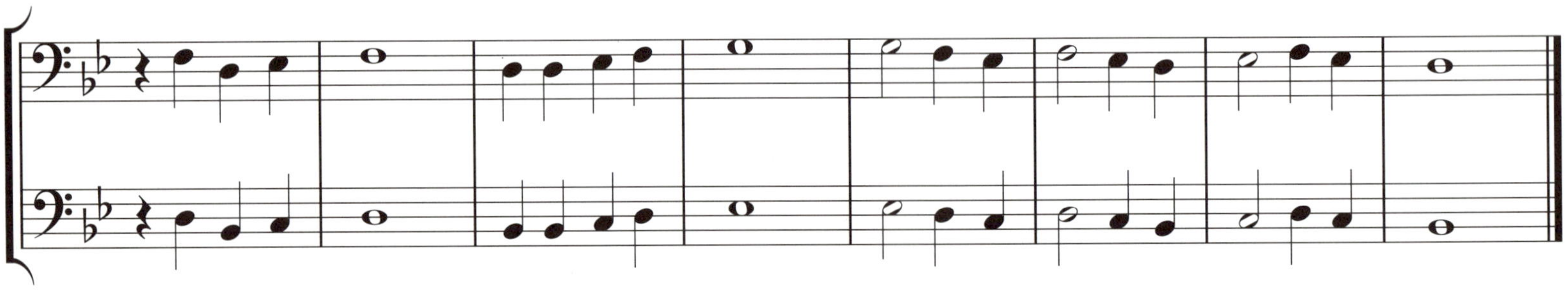

Play Premier Technique Lines 5 and 6 on page 44.

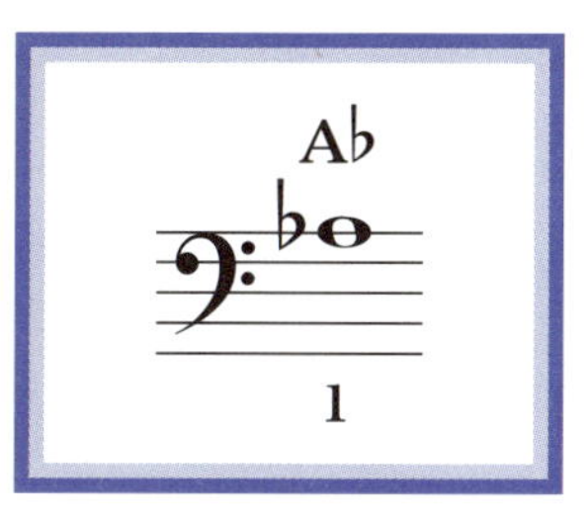

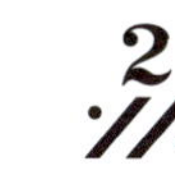

Repeat the 2 previous measures.

PICK-UP NOTE(S)

Note(s) before the first measure of a song

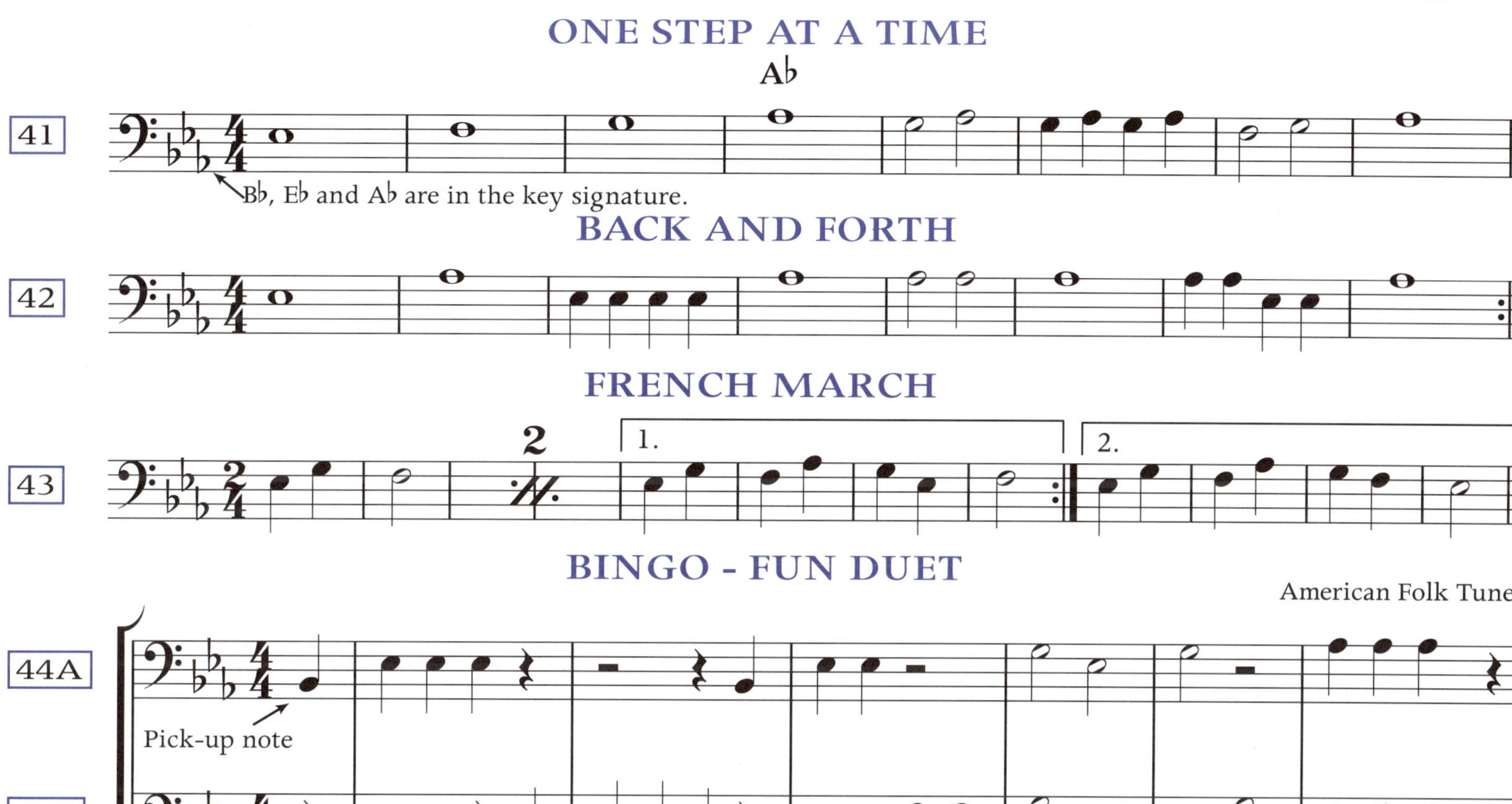

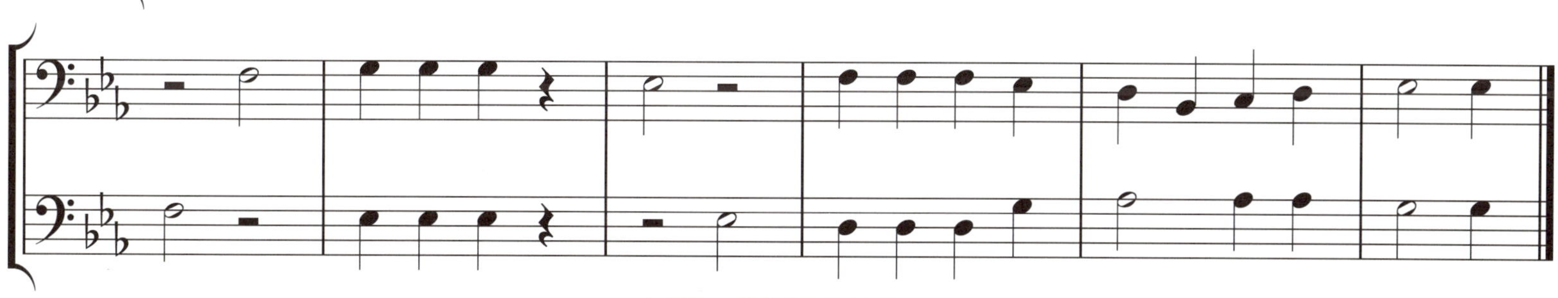

AIR CONTEST

1 2 3 4 5 6 7 8 9 10 11 12 13 14 15 16

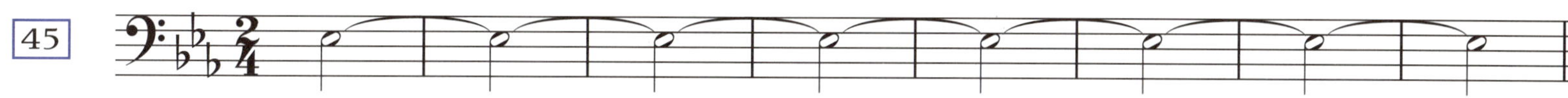

How far can you go in one breath? Circle the highest number you reach!

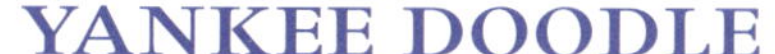

YANKEE DOODLE

Early American Tune

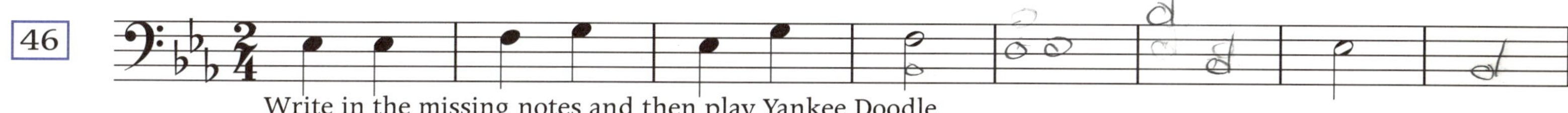

Write in the missing notes and then play Yankee Doodle.

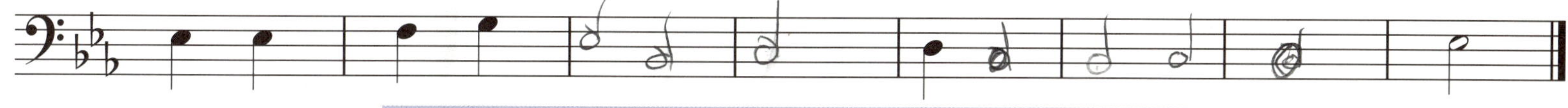

Play Premier Rhythm Lines 4 and 5 on page 42.

TIME SIGNATURE

3 = 3 beats in a measure
4 = quarter note receives 1 beat

DOTTED HALF NOTE

A dotted half note receives 3 beats in $\frac{3}{4}$ and $\frac{4}{4}$ time. The dot adds half the value of the note.

SLUR

A slur is a curved line that connects notes of different pitches. Tongue the first note only.

COUNTING THREE

47

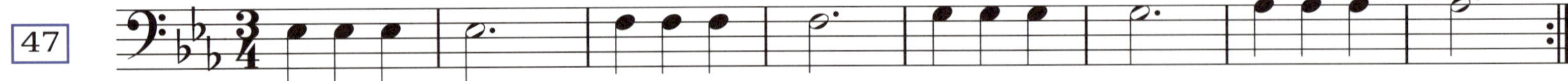

DOWN IN THE VALLEY

Kentucky Mountain Song

48

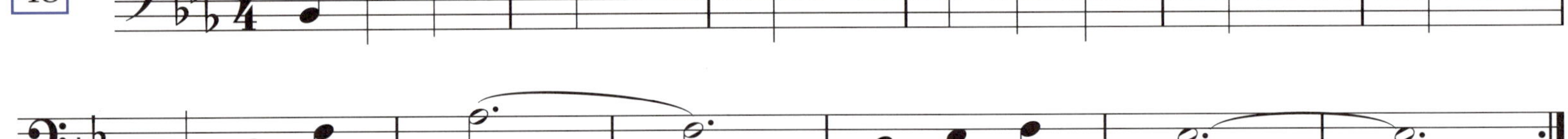

WALTZ FOR TWO

Ed Sueta

49A
49B

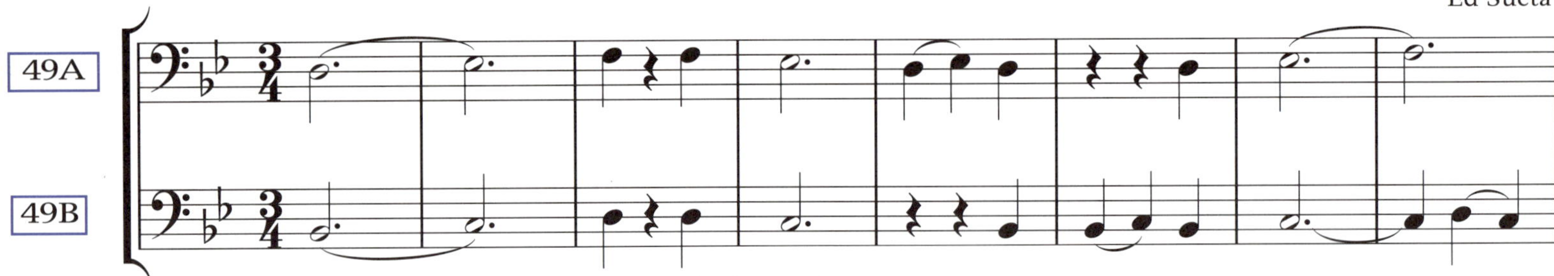

Keep your air steady and even during all slurs and ties.

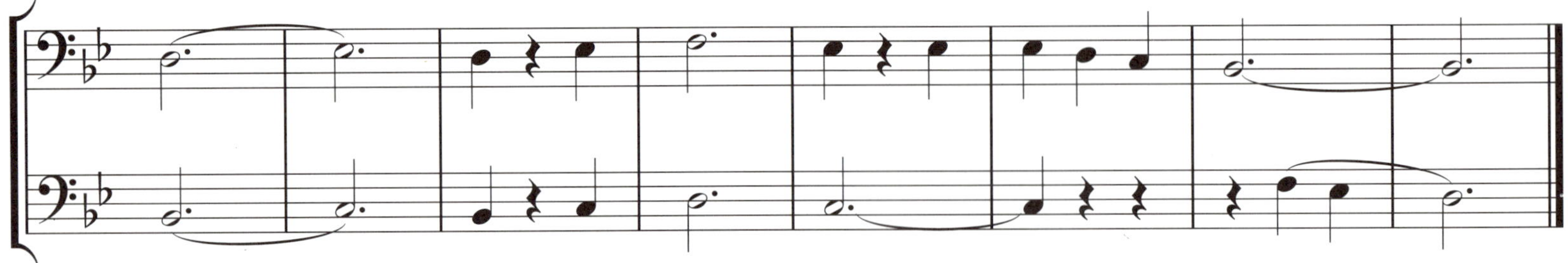

MARCH OF THE VICTORS

Football Song

50

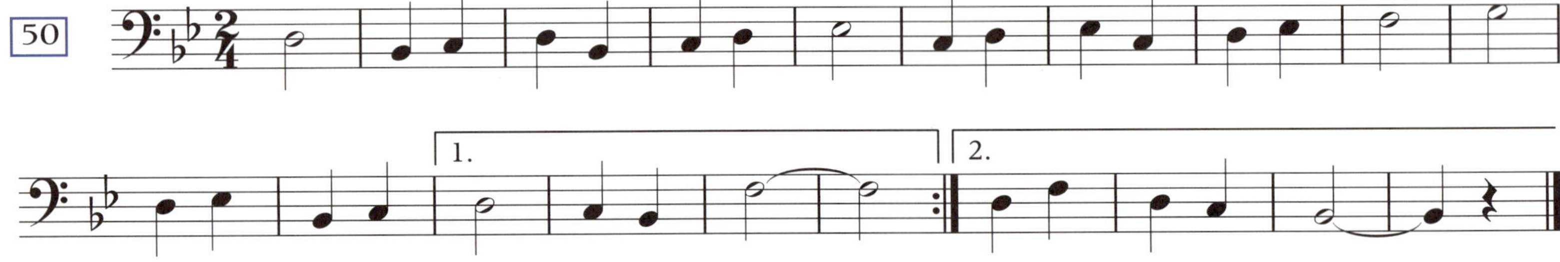

Play Premier Technique Lines 7 and 8 on page 44.

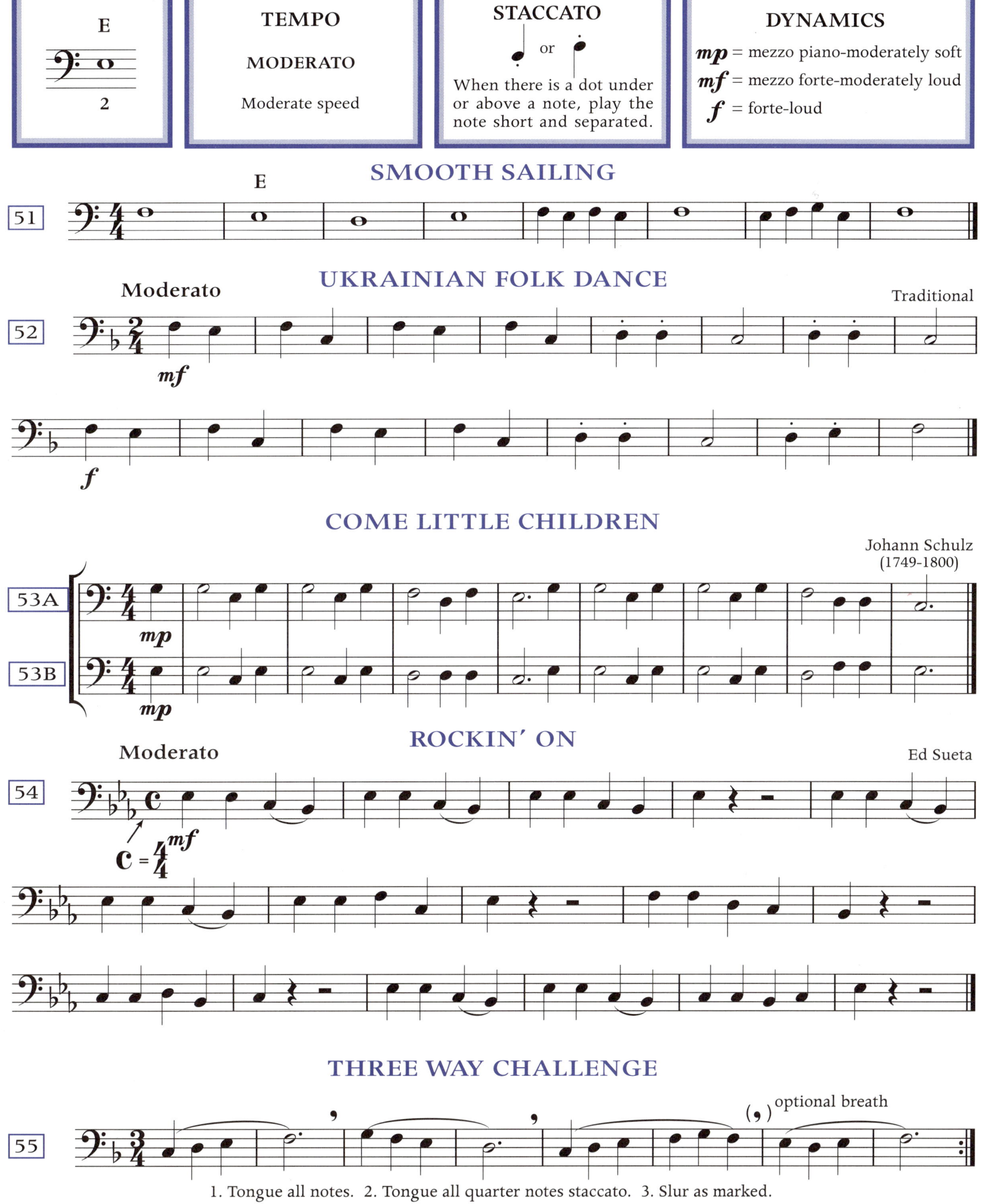

Play Premier Rhythm Lines 6 and 7 on page 42.

EIGHTH NOTE RHYTHM PATTERNS

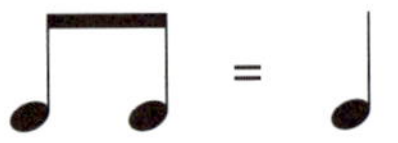

Two eighth notes equal one quarter note.

Each eighth note receives ½ of a beat in 2/4, 3/4 and 4/4 time.

1

2

3

4

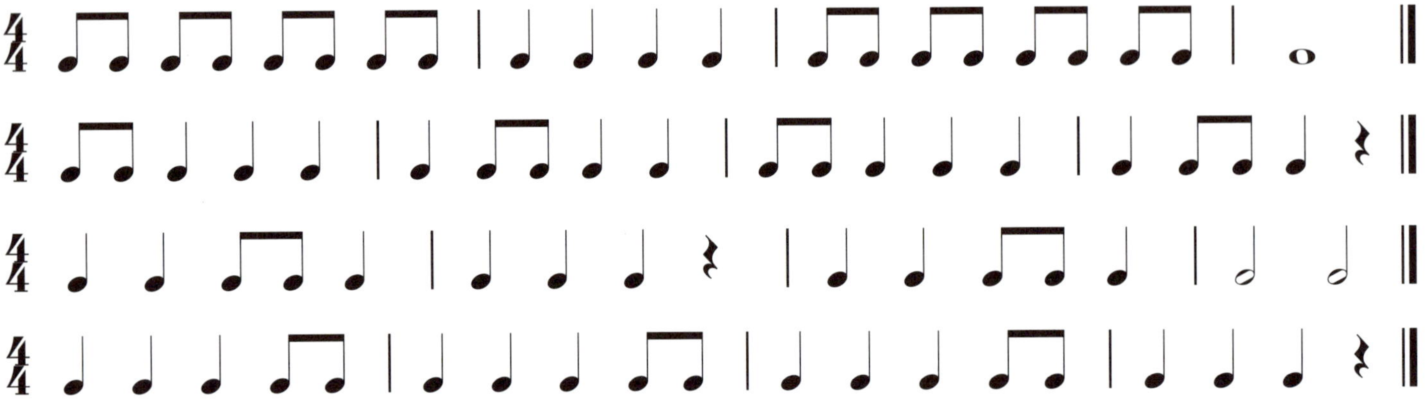

EIGHTH NOTE PATTERNS

56

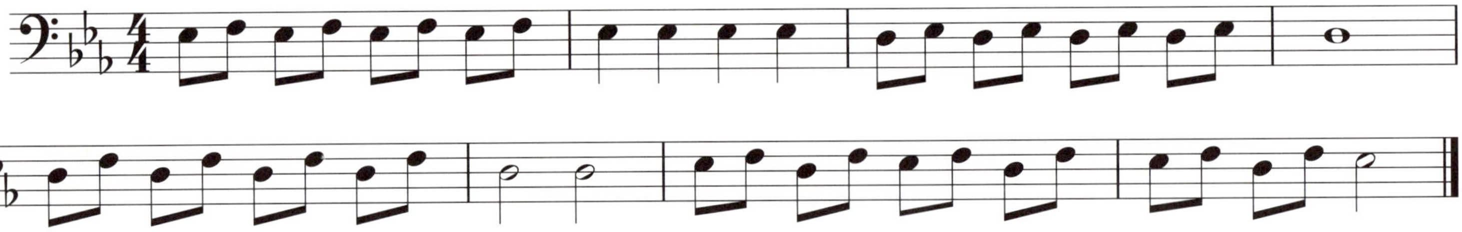

MEXICAN FIESTA!

Moderato

Sierra Madre Region

57

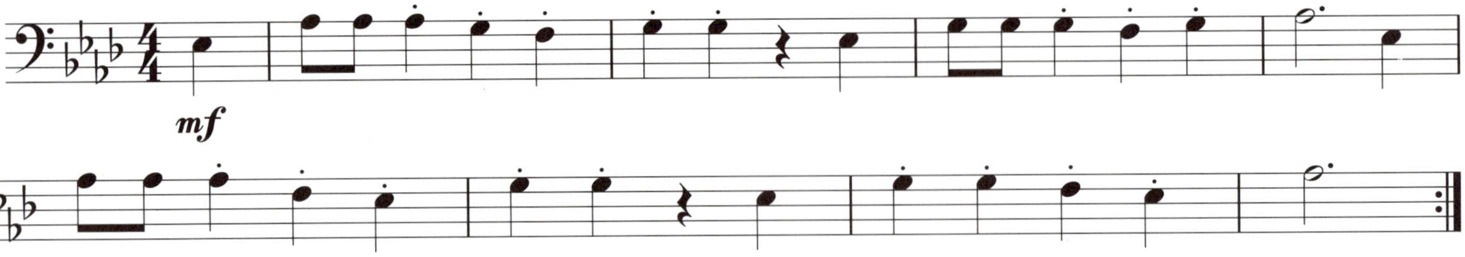

mf

SQUARE DANCE

Lively

Ed Sueta

58

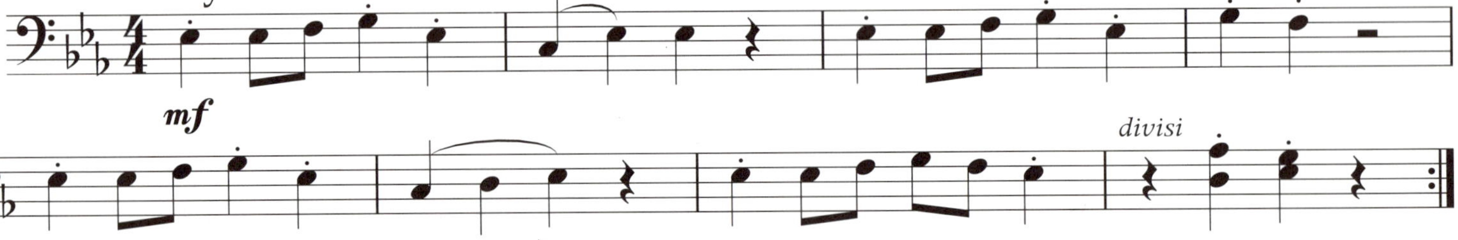

mf

divisi

Play Premier Technique Lines 9 and 10 on page 44.

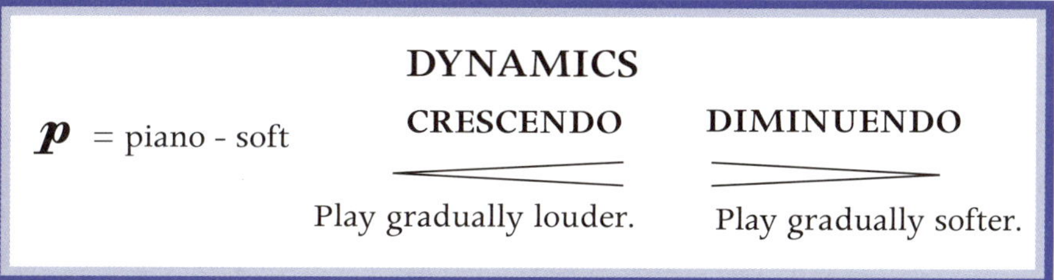

EXCERPT

A part of a composition

HARMONY

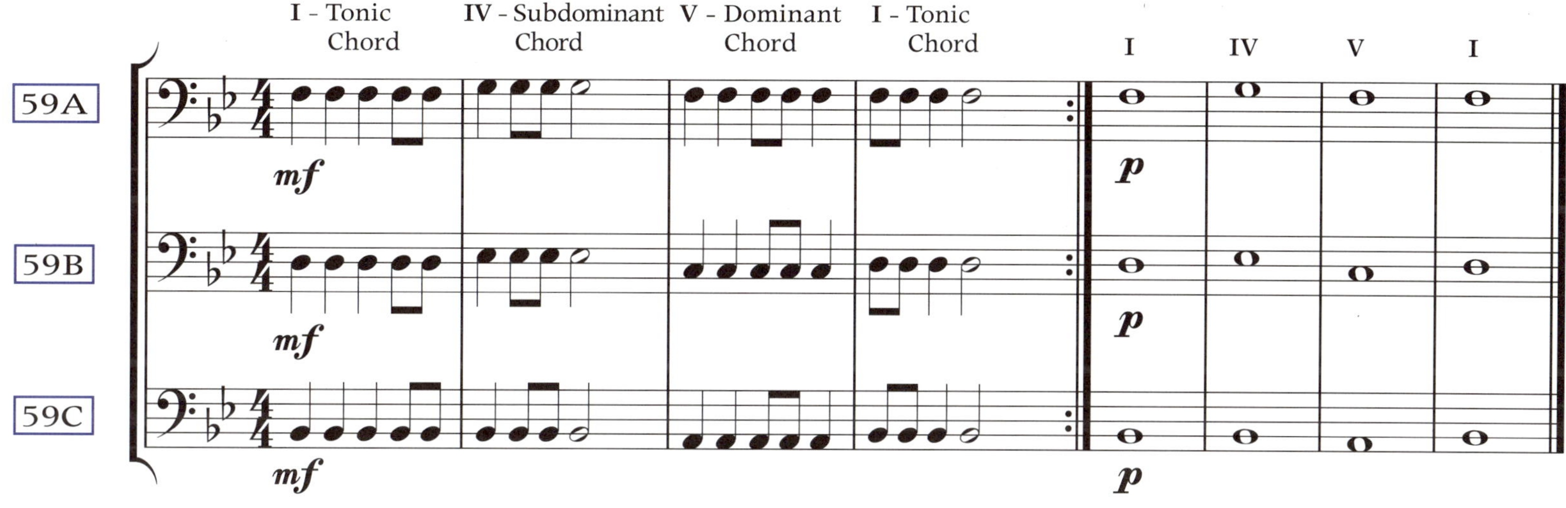

SEA SONG

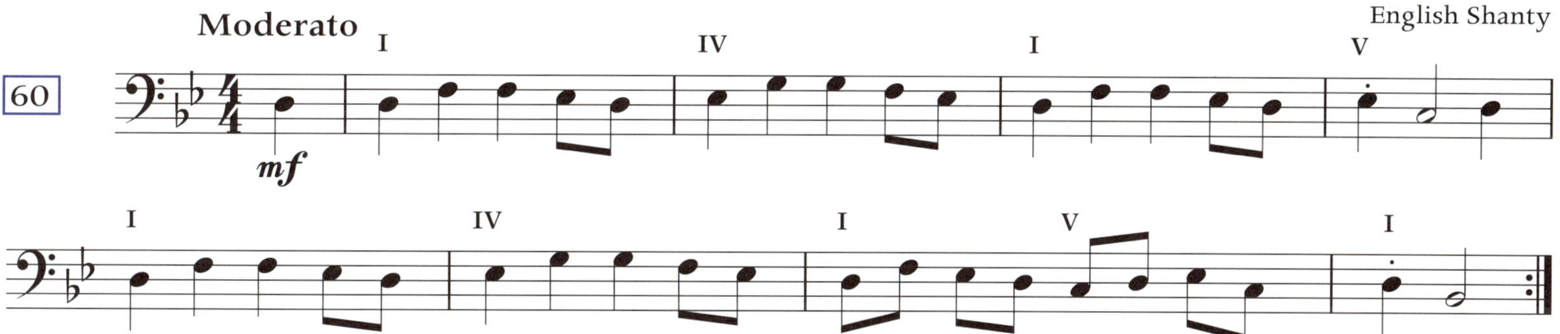

DANCE OF THE REED FLUTES

EXCERPT FROM THE NUTCRACKER SUITE

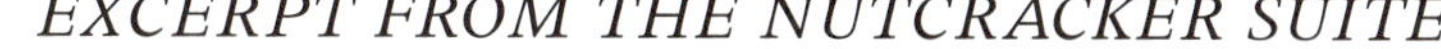

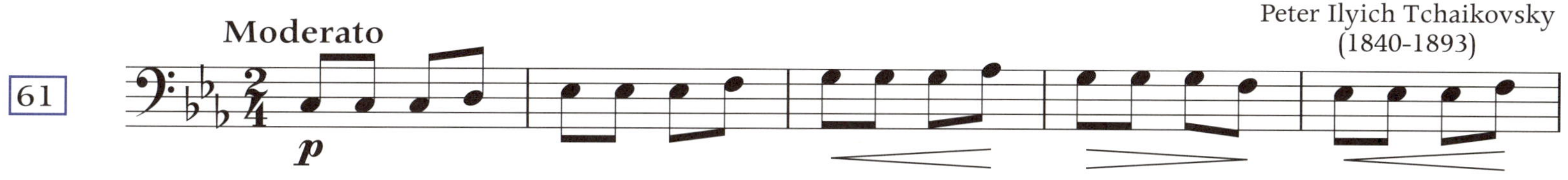

Quick breaths are necessary. As you breathe in, do not lift your shoulders.

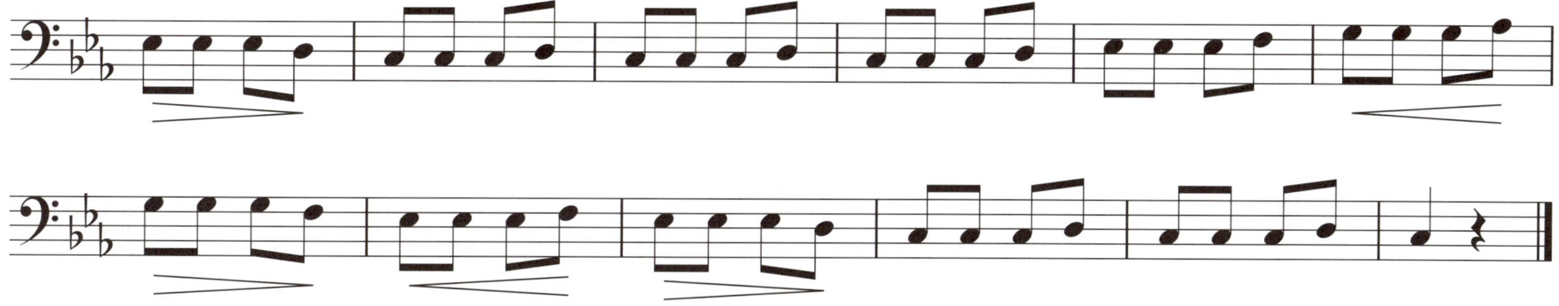

Play Premier Rhythm Lines 8, 9 and 10 on page 42.

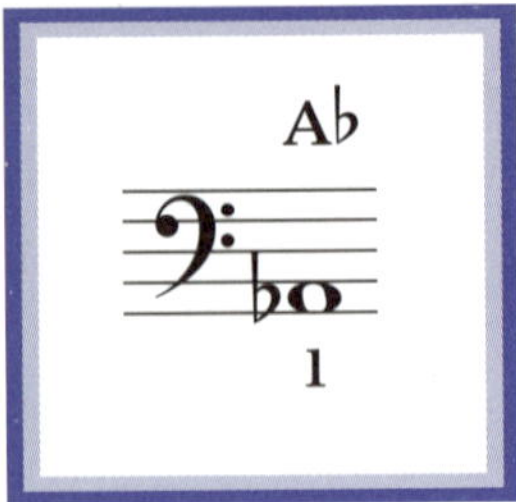

ACCIDENTAL

An accidental is a sharp, flat or natural which is not in the key signature. It lasts for 1 measure.

TEMPO

ANDANTE
Moderately slow

ALLEGRO
Fast and lively

FERMATA

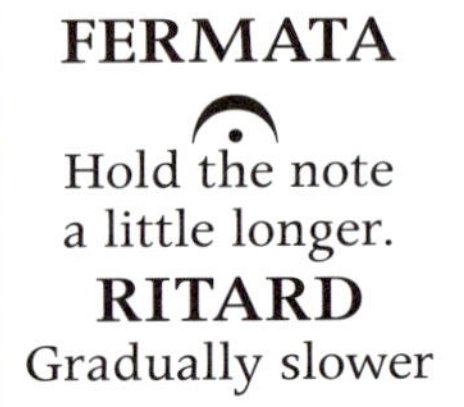

Hold the note a little longer.

RITARD
Gradually slower

SLOW AND ACCURATE

62 A♭

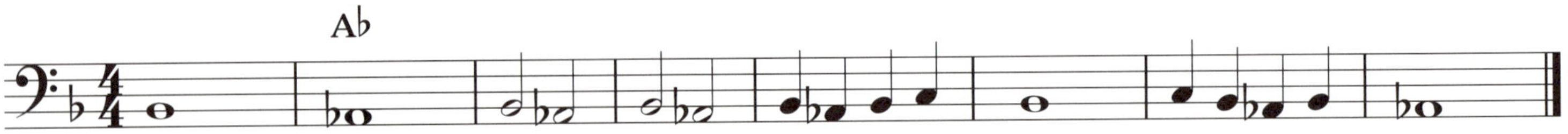

LIL LIZA JANE

Moderato — American Folk Tune

63 *mp* *f*

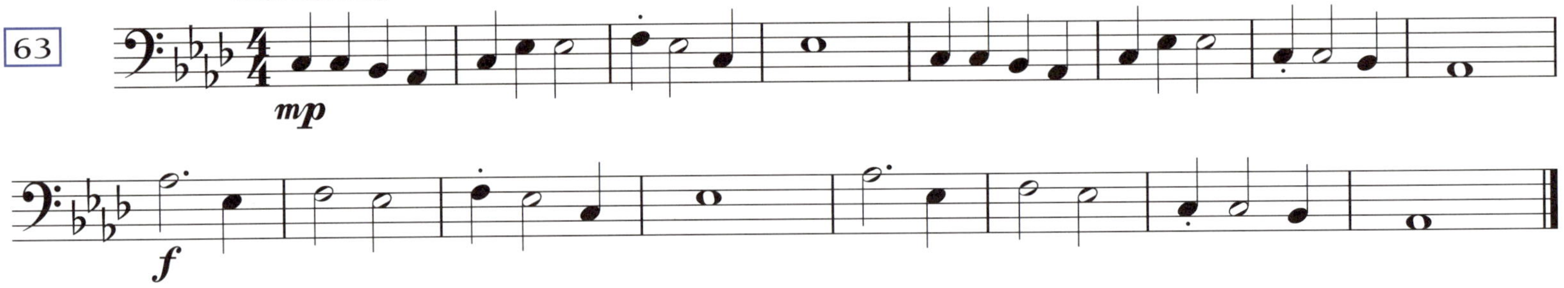

CARIBBEAN CHA CHA

Moderato — Ed Sueta

64 *mp* accidental — The natural sign (♮) cancels the flat until the next measure.

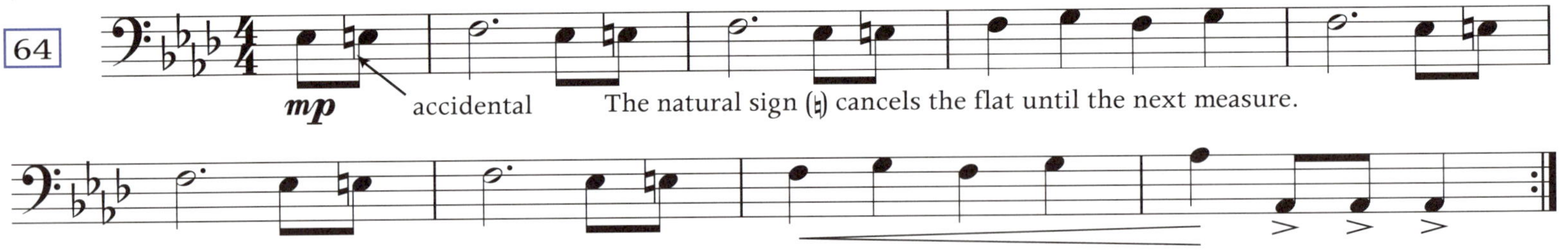

WAYFARING STRANGER

Andante — Folk Ballad

65 *mp* *ritard*

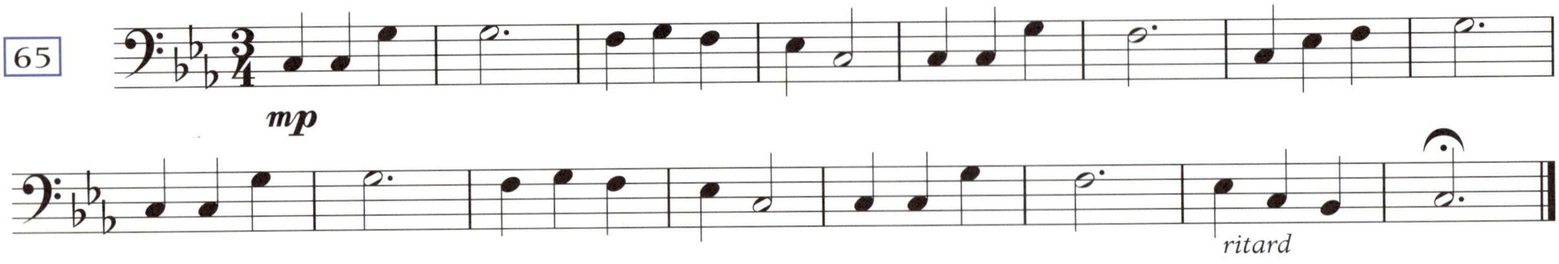

THEME FROM MIDSUMMER NIGHT'S DREAM

Felix Mendelssohn
(1809-1847)

Allegro

66 *mp*

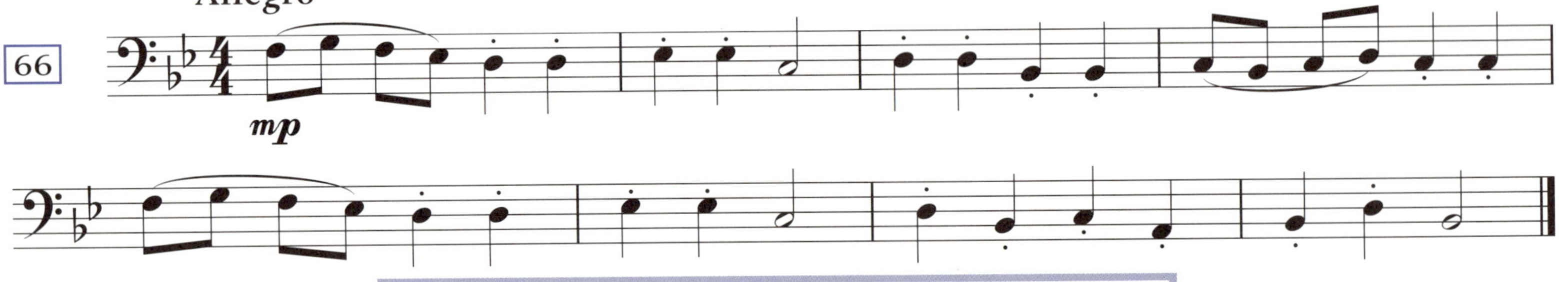

Play Premier Rhythm Lines 11 and 12 on page 43.

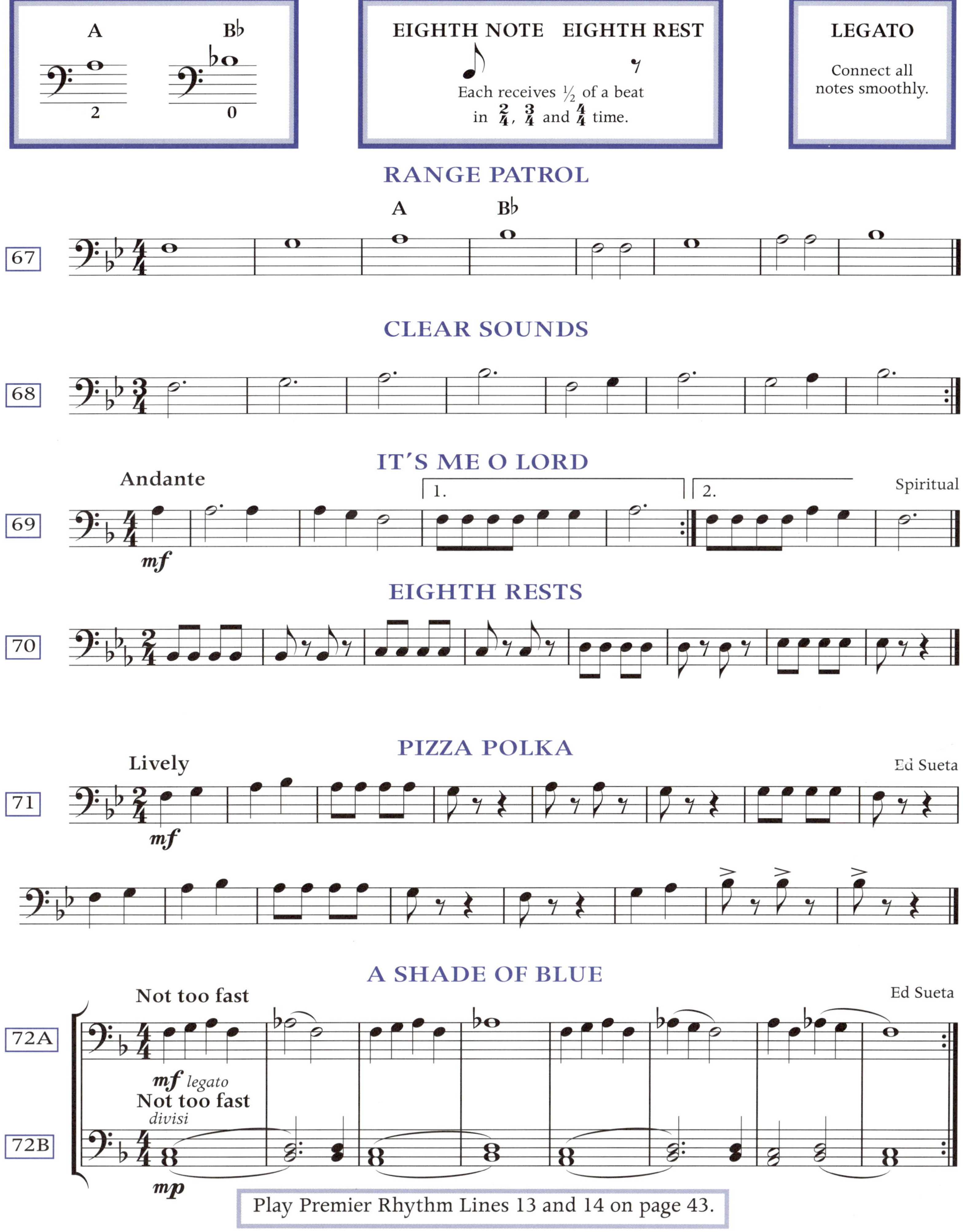

Play Premier Rhythm Lines 13 and 14 on page 43.

Play Premier Technique Lines 11 and 12 on page 45.

MARCH TO THE DRY GULCH

Jim Engebretson

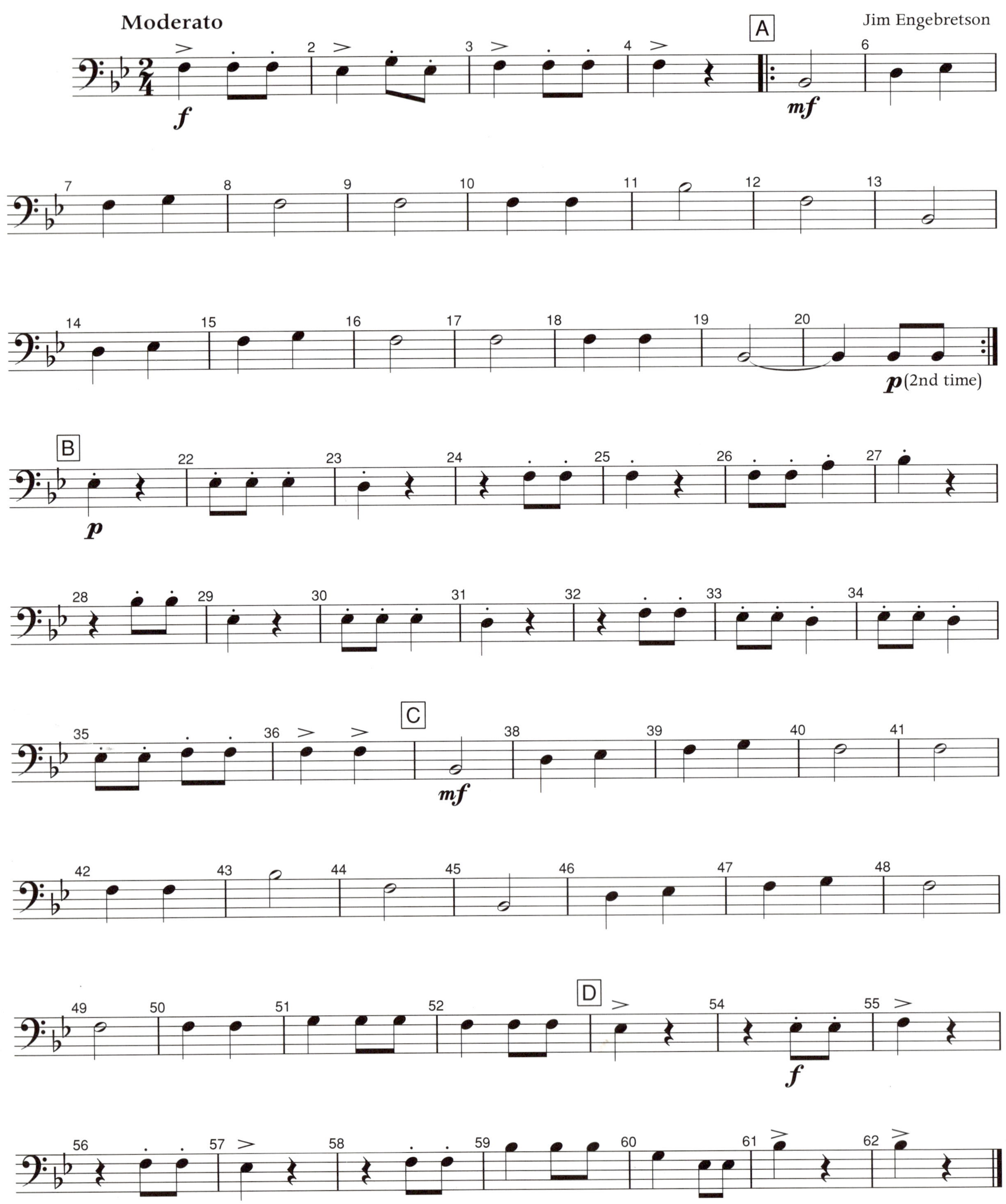

TEMPO
CON SPIRITO
With Spirit

TAKE YOUR TIME

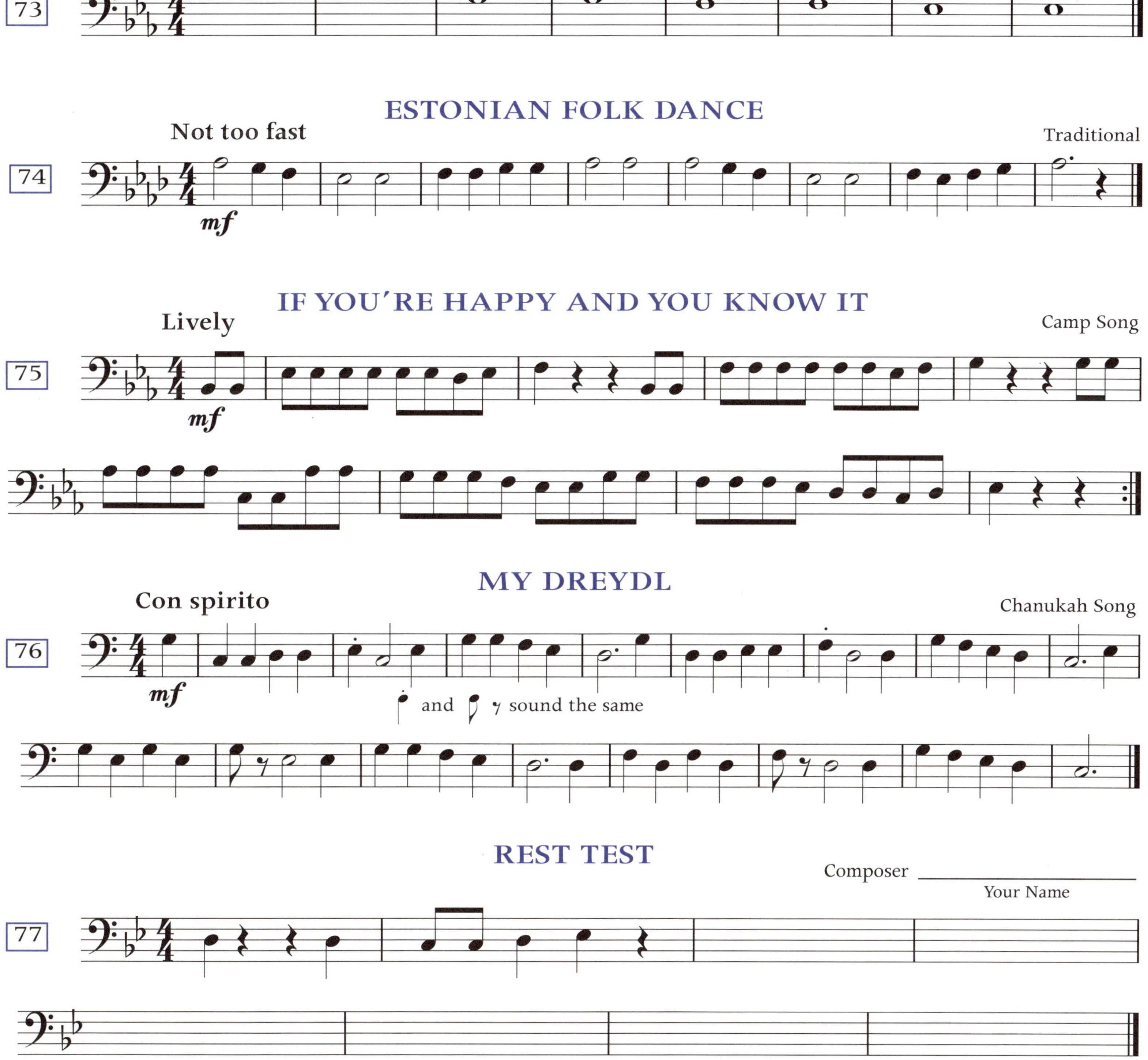

Complete this Rest Test and then play your composition.

Play Premier Rhythm Lines 15 and 16 on page 43.

DA CAPO AL FINE (D.C. AL FINE)

Go back to the beginning and play to the *Fine*.

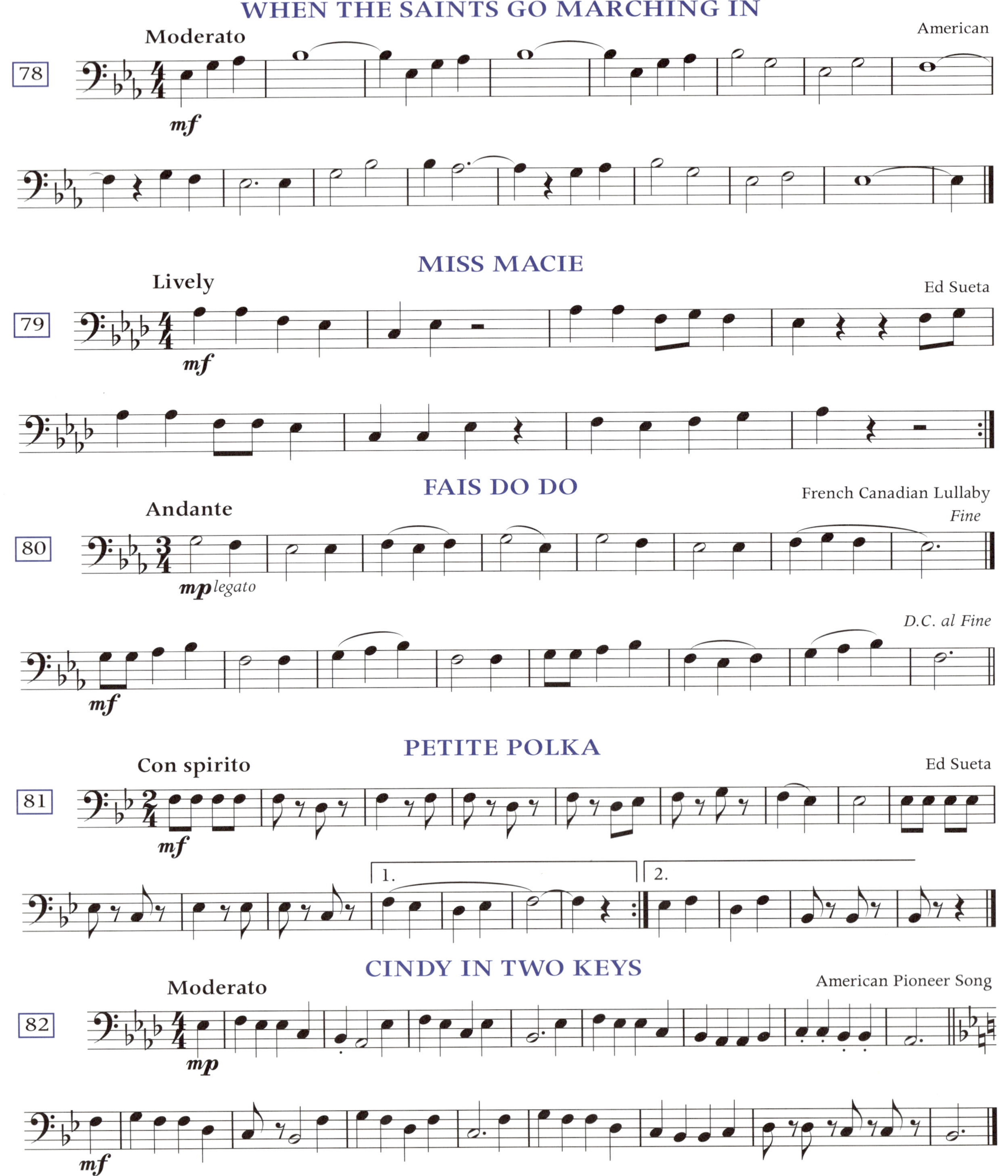

CHI CHI CHA CHA

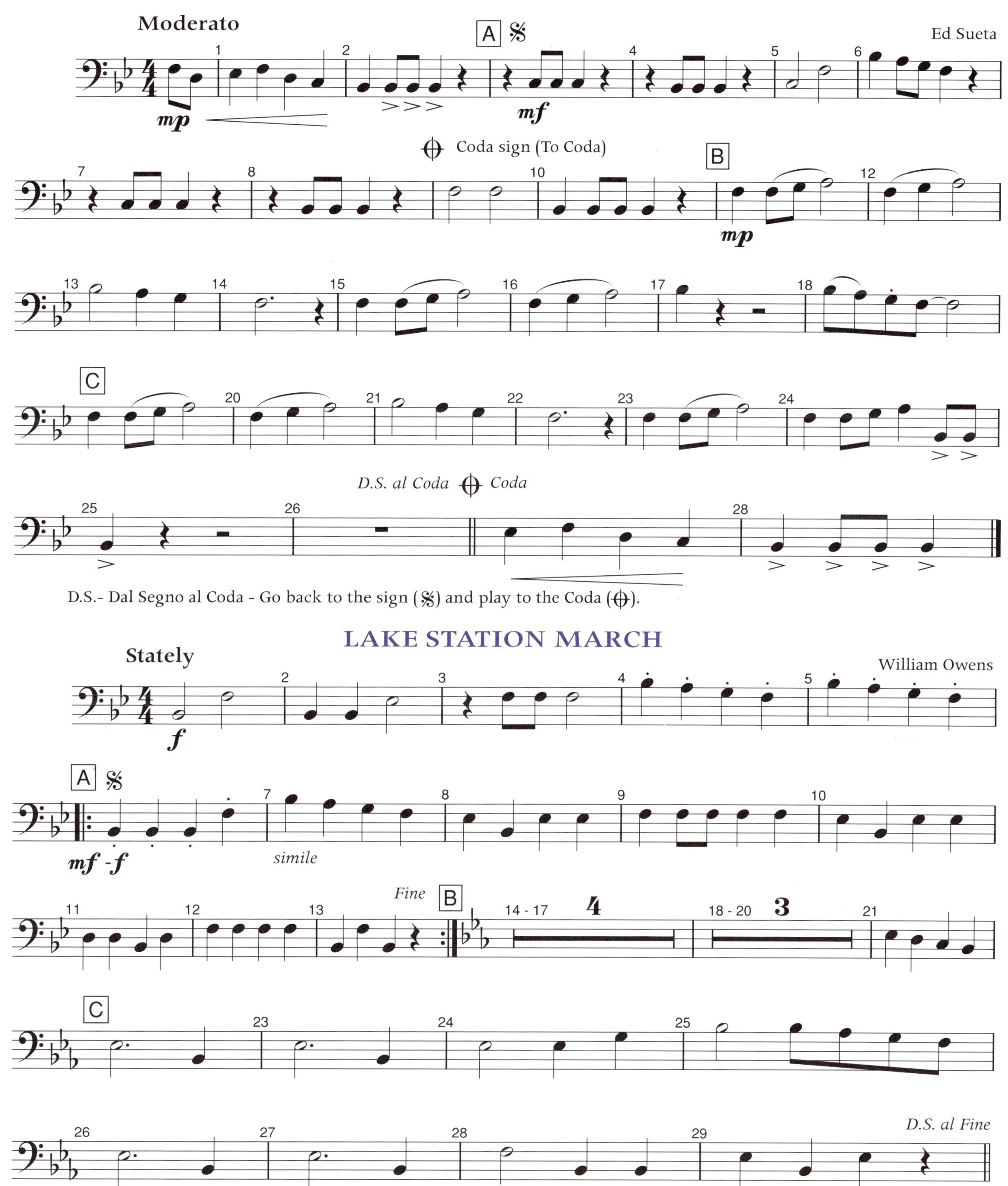

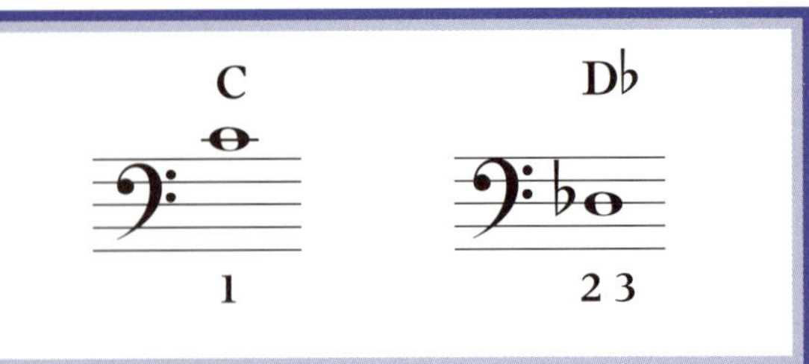

DAL SEGNO AL FINE (D.S. AL FINE)

Go back to the sign (𝄋) and play to the *Fine*.

LONG TONES

83

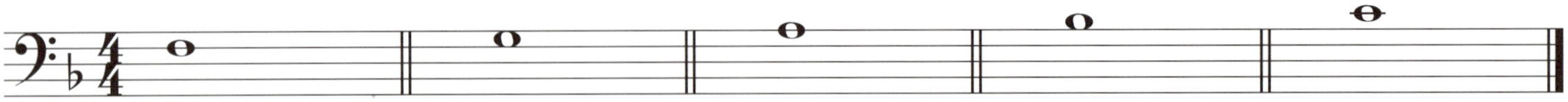

C

RANGE CONTROL

84

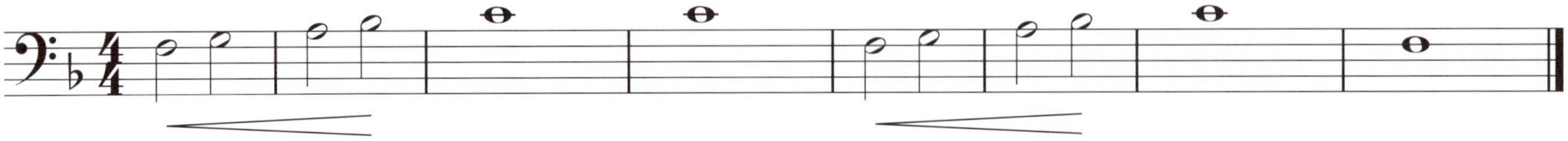

INDIAN CHANT

Slowly

Native American

85

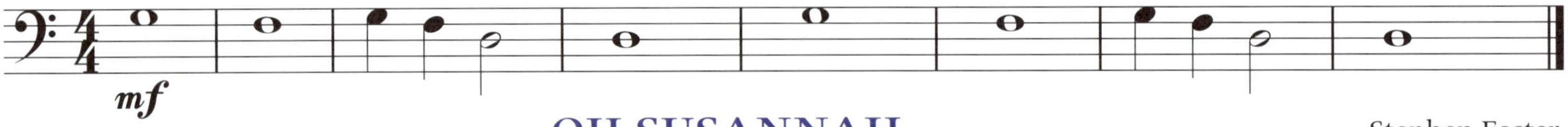

mf

OH SUSANNAH

Lively

Stephen Foster (1826-1864)

86

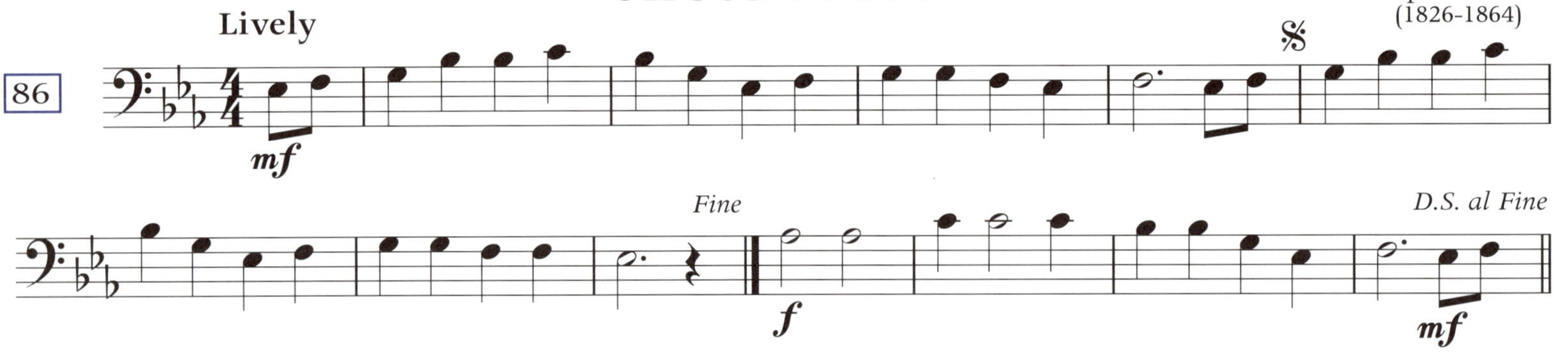

mf

Fine

D.S. al Fine

f

mf

JULIE'S BLUES

Moderato

Ed Sueta

87

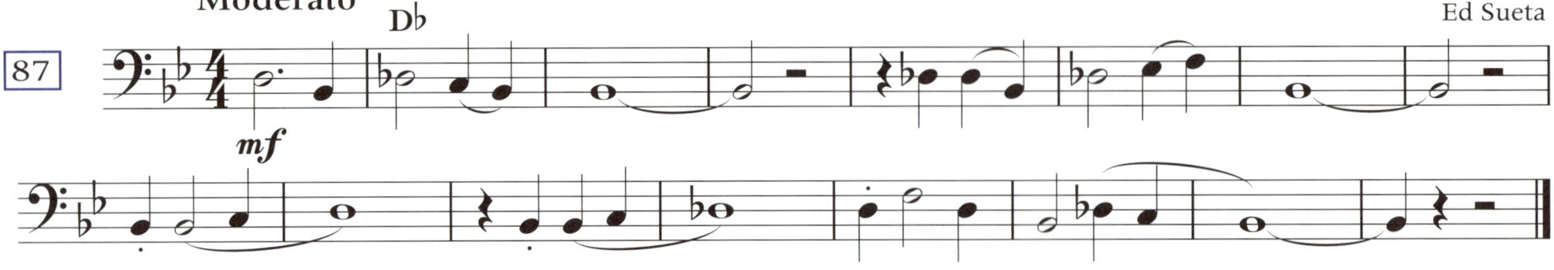

D♭

mf

UP ON THE HOUSE TOP

Moderato

Traditional Christmas Song

88

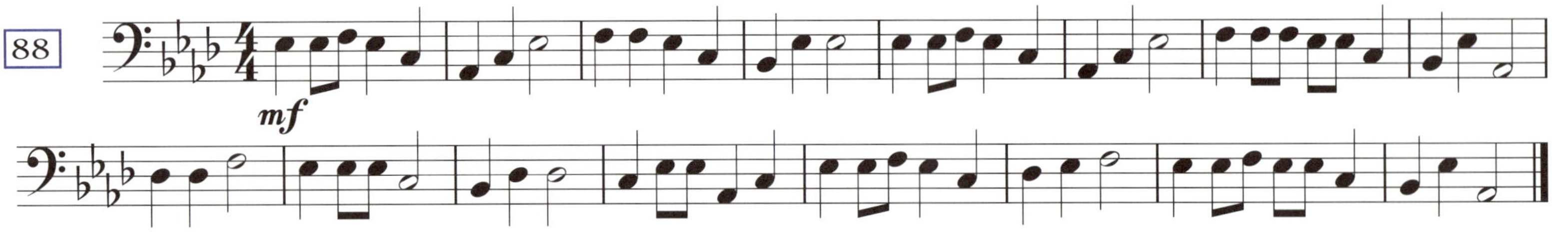

mf

Play Premier Technique Lines 13 and 14 on page 45.

TEMPO

ALLEGRETTO

Moderately fast

CLARINETS FLYING HIGH

89

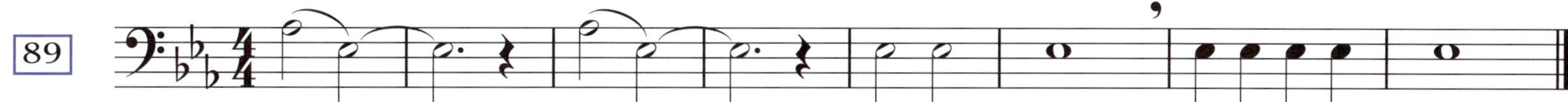

SECOND FLIGHT

90

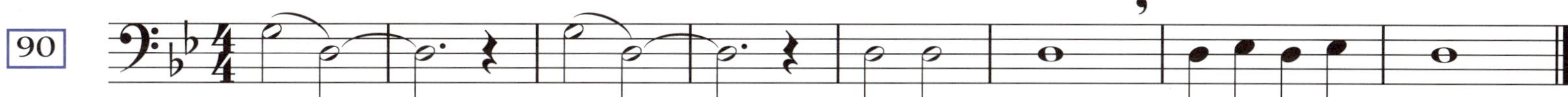

SAFE LANDING

91

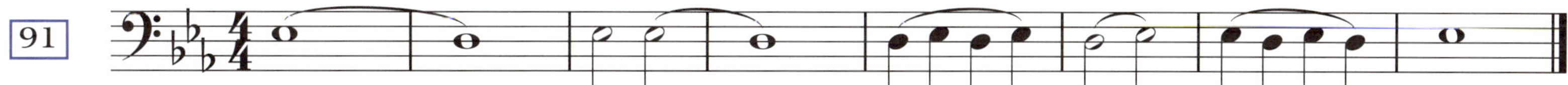

THIRD FLIGHT

92

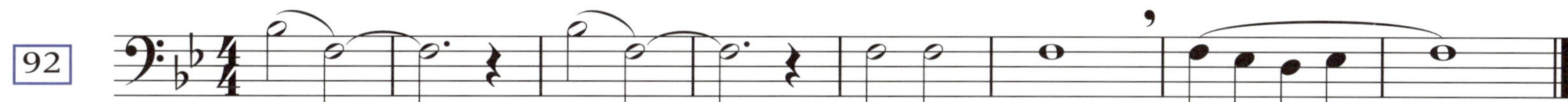

STEADY DOES IT

93

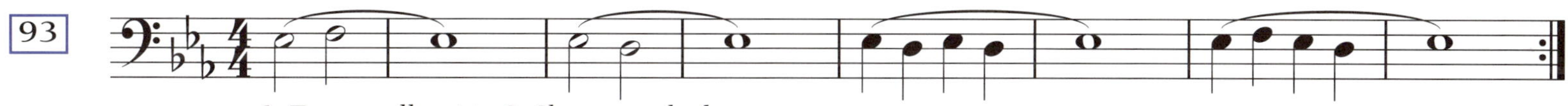

1. Tongue all notes. 2. Slur as marked.

SMOOTH CONNECTIONS

94

mf

PORTUGUESE WALTZ

Algarve Region

95A

95B

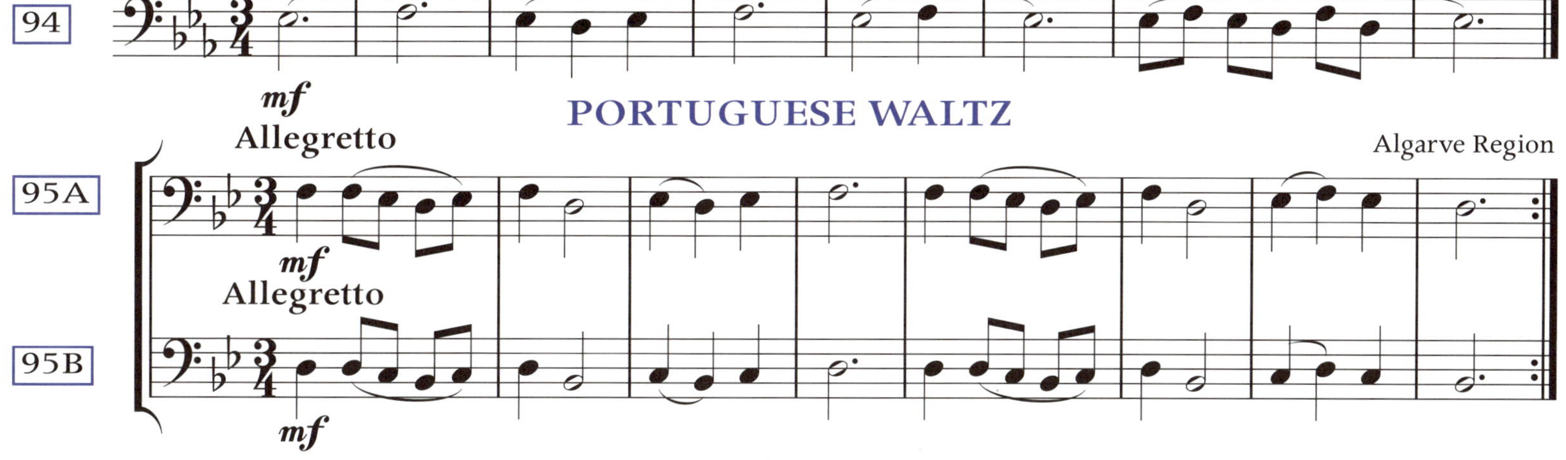

FOR BARITONES

96

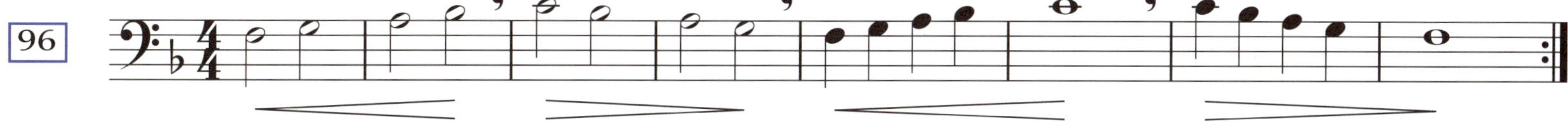

When this line becomes easy to play, increase your speed.

AIR CONTROL

Write in seconds

97

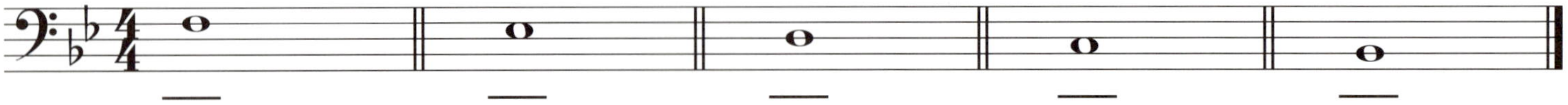

How many seconds can you hold each note?

SMOOTH AND EVEN

98

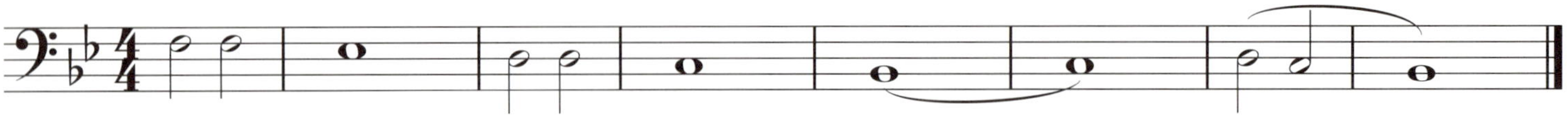

ALPINE MOUNTAIN SONG

Not too fast

Swiss Folk Song

99

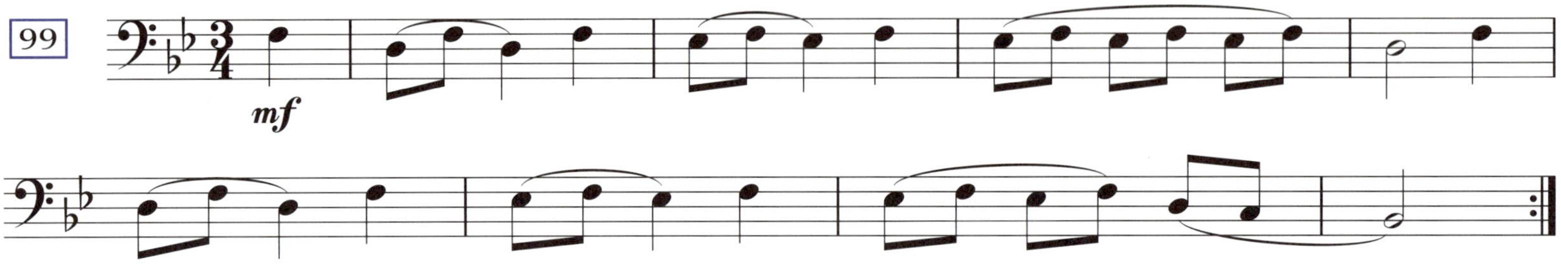

mf

WINTER GOOD-BYE

German Melody

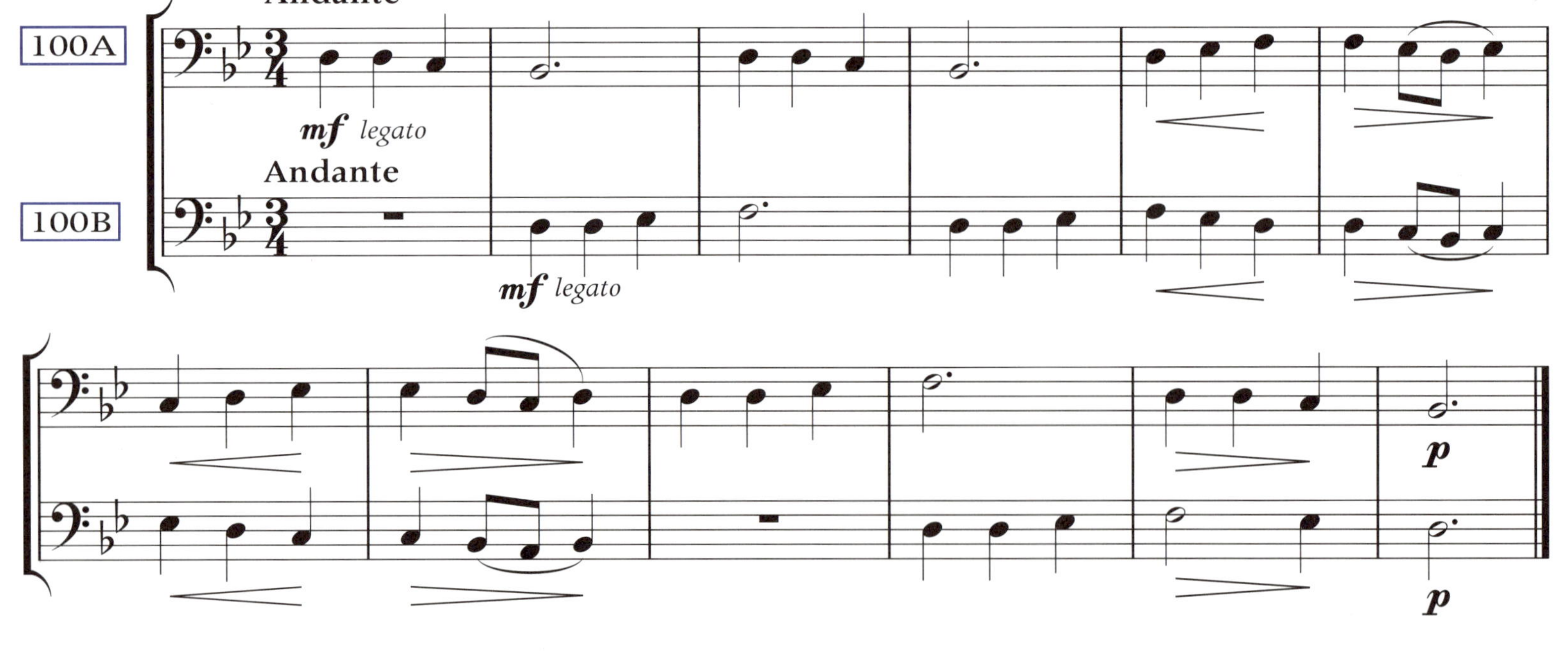

FOR BARITONES

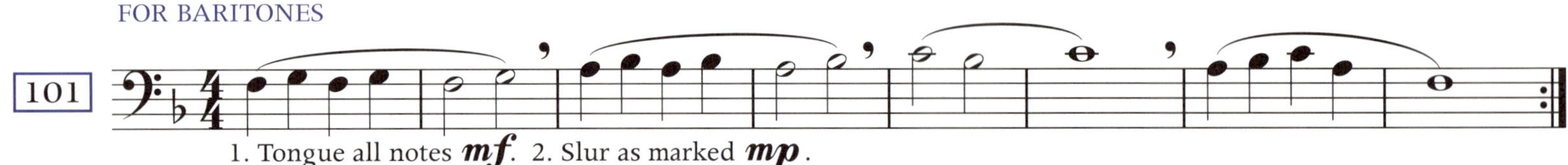

Play Premier Technique Lines 15 and 16 on page 45.

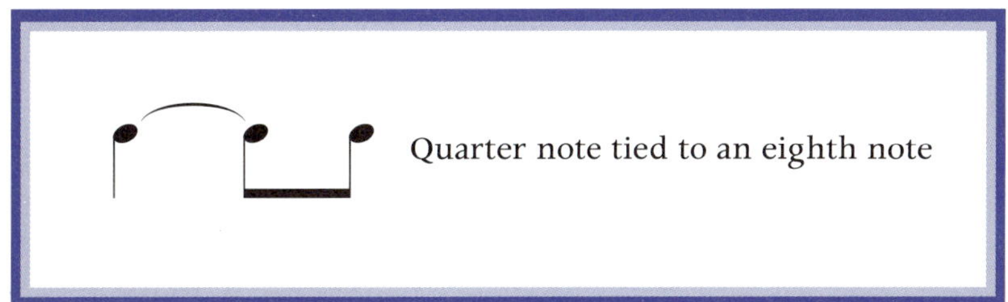

ALL TIED UP

102

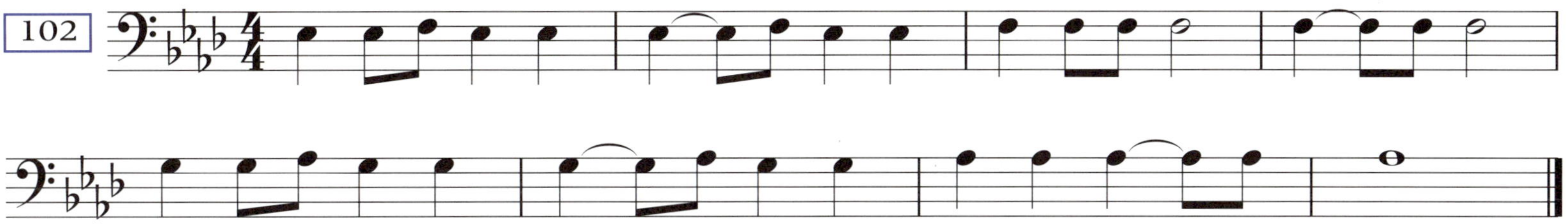

JINGLE BELLS

James S. Pierpont (1822-1893)

Moderato

103

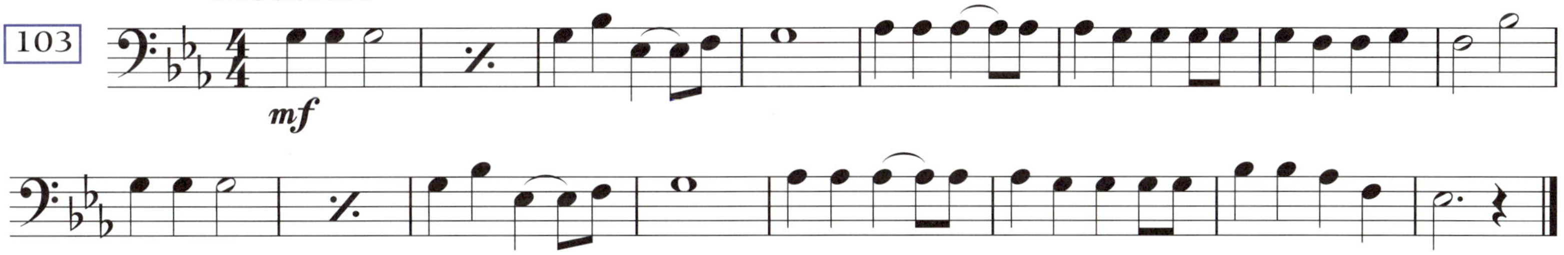

mf

THEME FROM THE NINTH SYMPHONY

Ludwig van Beethoven (1770-1827)

Moderato

104

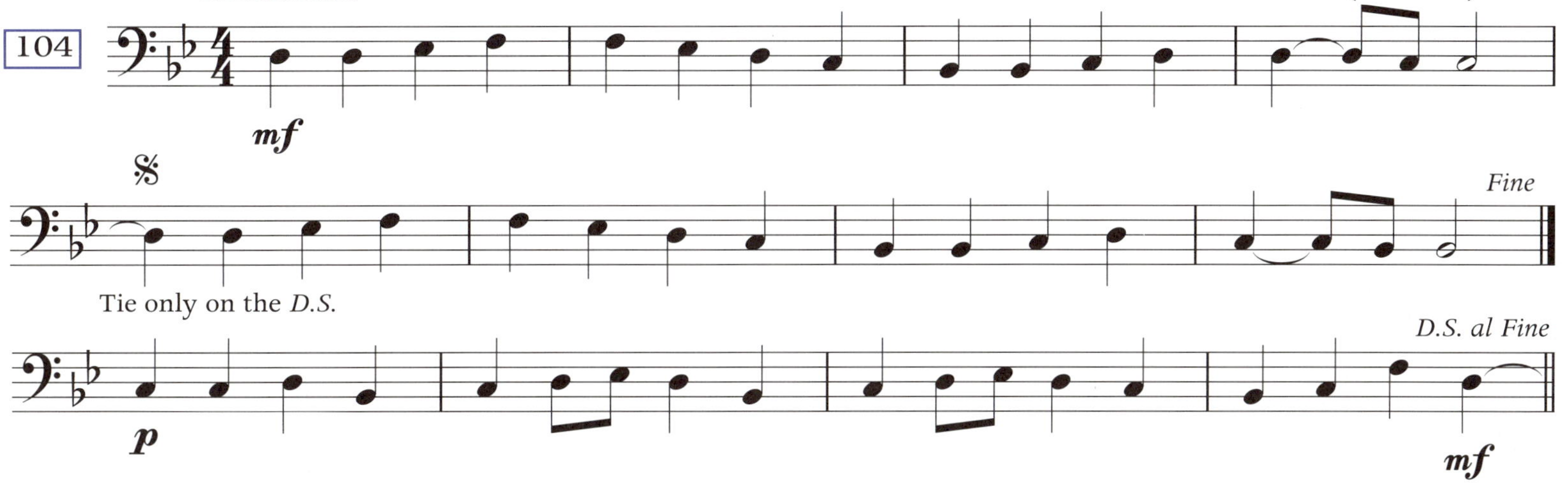

mf

Fine

Tie only on the *D.S.*

D.S. al Fine

p

mf

SOURWOOD MOUNTAIN

Appalachian Folk Song

Lively

105

mf

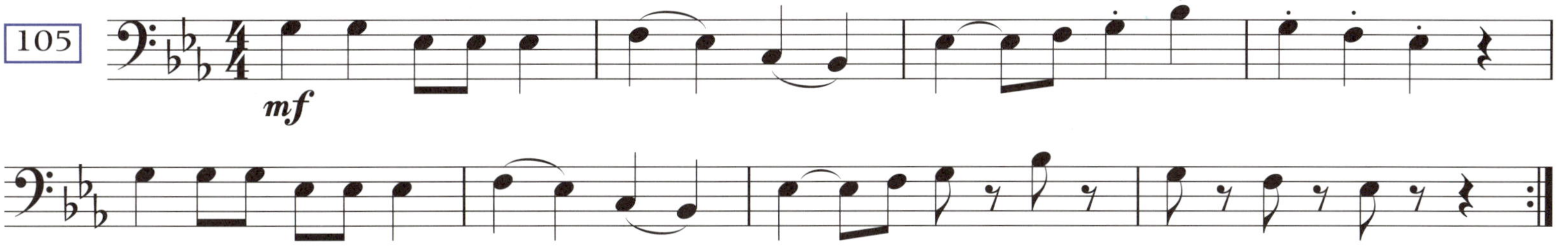

Play Premier Technique Lines 17 and 18 on page 45.

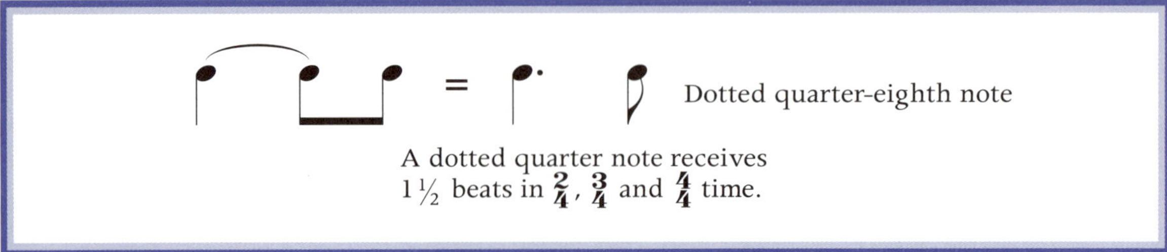

COUNTING DOTS

106

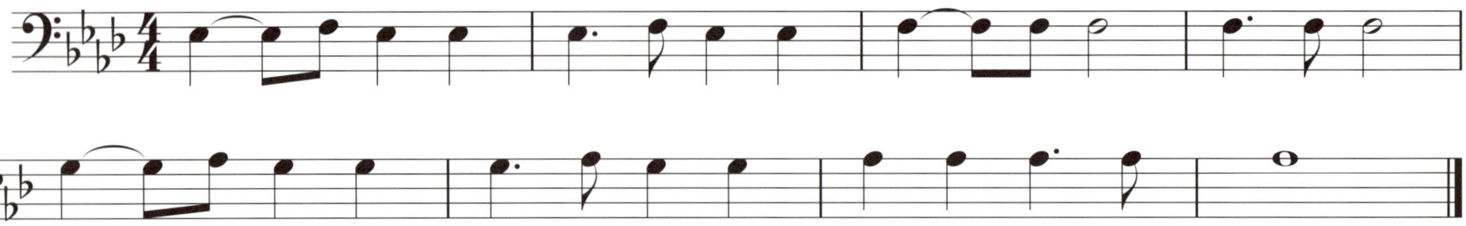

TWO SPIRITUALS

STEAL AWAY

Andante

107

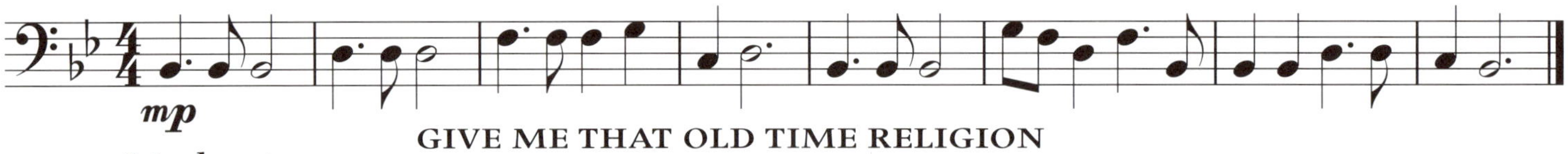

mp

GIVE ME THAT OLD TIME RELIGION

Moderato

108

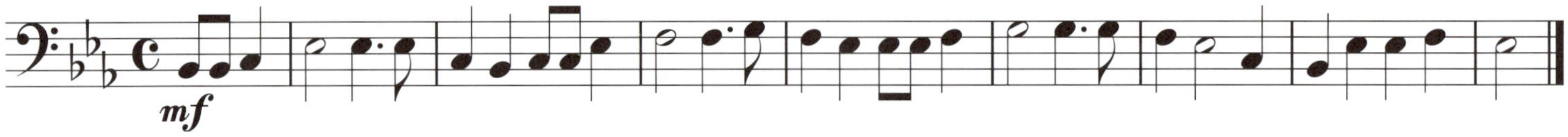

mf

TYROLEAN DANCE

Allegro

Austrian Folk Dance

109

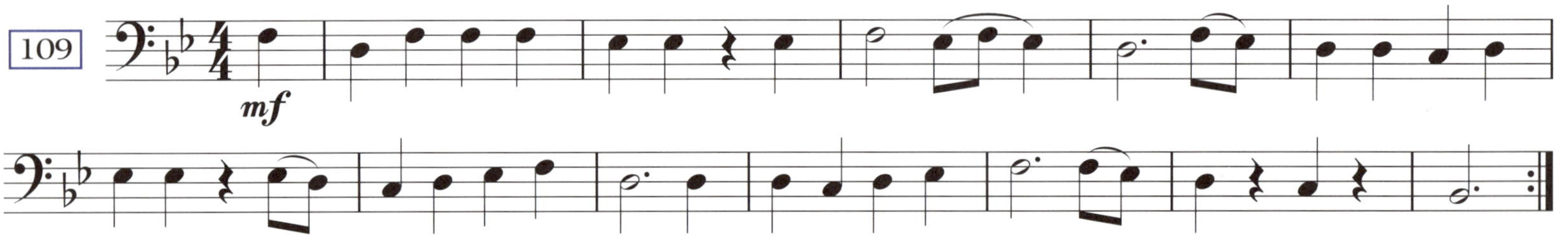

mf

THE OVERLANDER

*THE QUEENSLAND DROVER**

Lively

Australian Folk Song

110

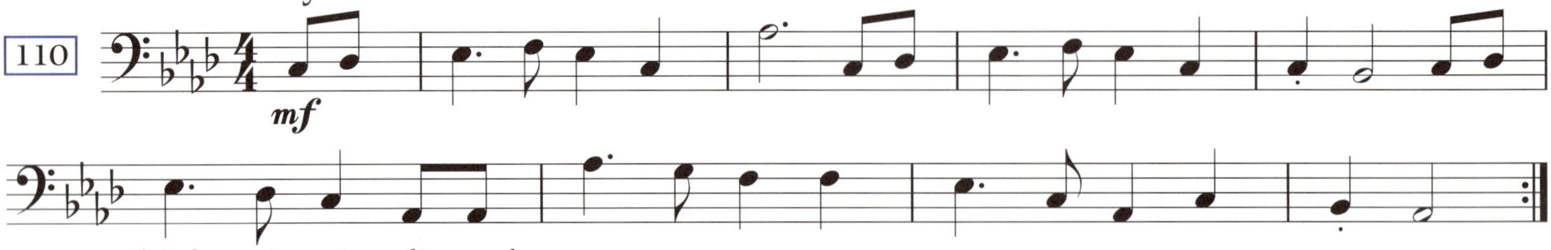

mf

* A drover is an Australian cowboy.

111

How fast can you say the notes and rests?

Fill in the number of beats ___ ___ ___ ___ ___ ___ ___ ___ ___ ___

Play Premier Rhythm Lines 17 and 18 on page 43.

TYRANNOSAURUS REX STOMP

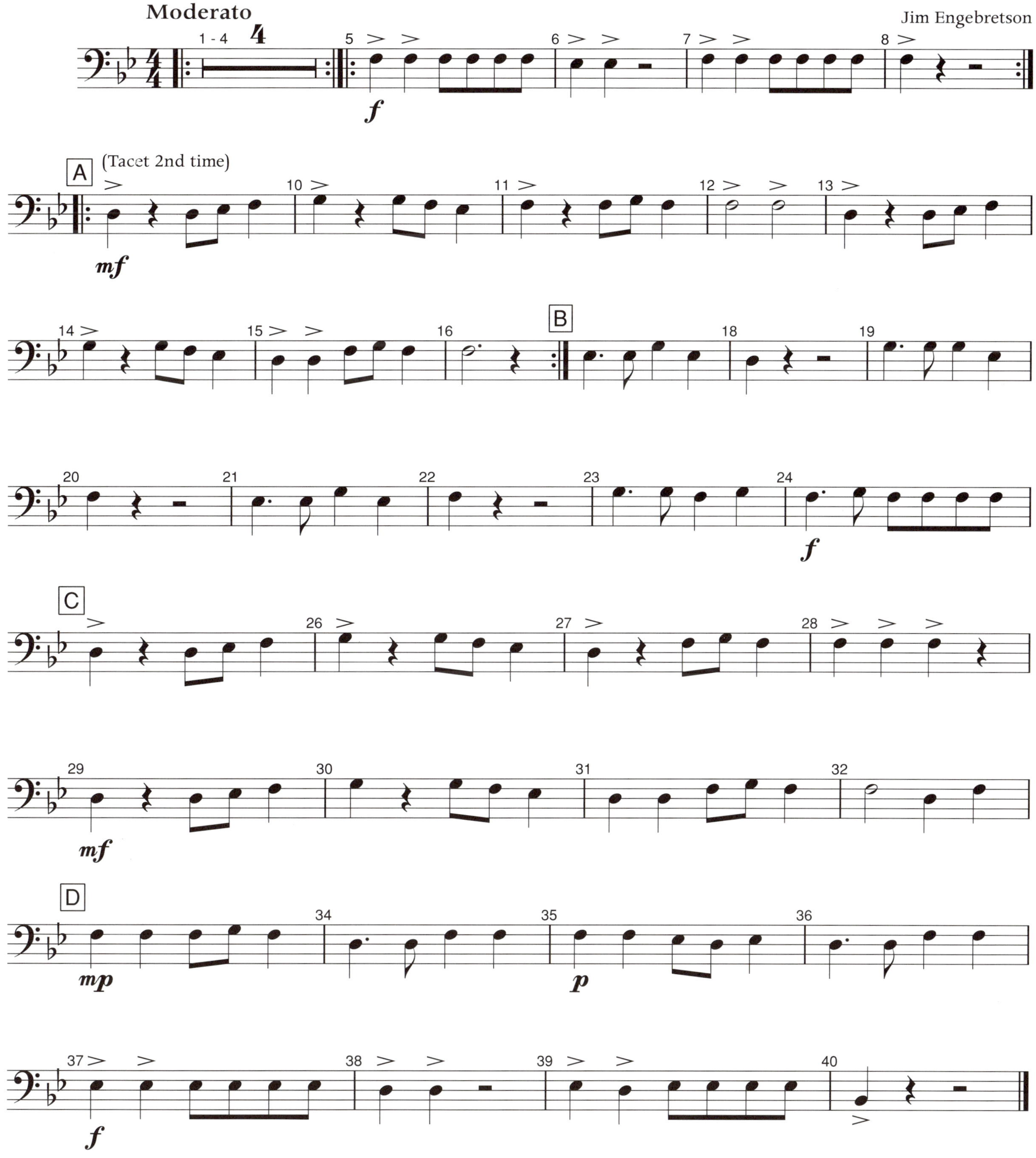

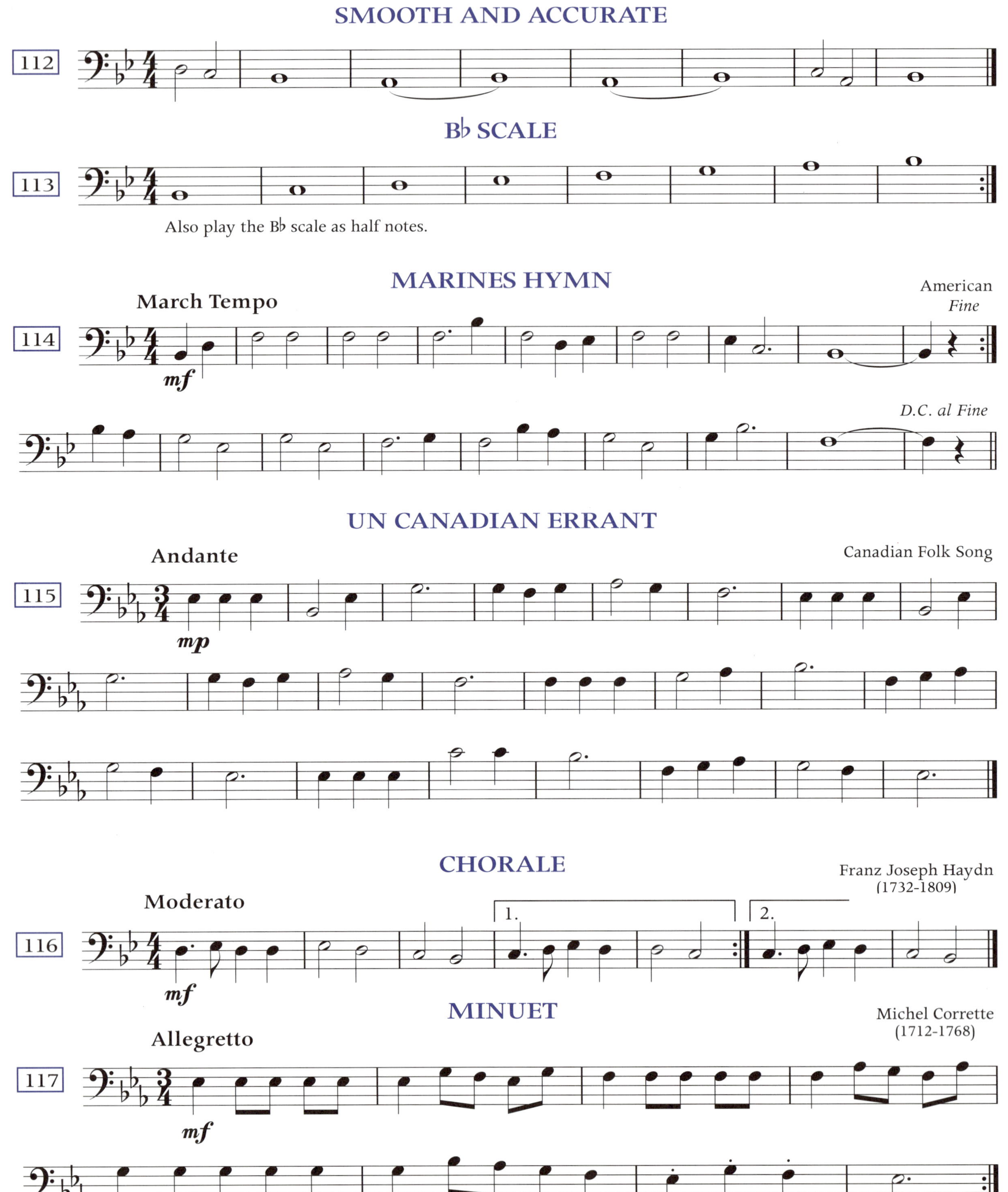
SMOOTH AND ACCURATE
112
B♭ SCALE
113
Also play the B♭ scale as half notes.
MARINES HYMN
American
March Tempo
Fine
114
mf
D.C. al Fine
UN CANADIAN ERRANT
Andante
Canadian Folk Song
115
mp
CHORALE
Franz Joseph Haydn
(1732-1809)
Moderato
1.
2.
116
mf
MINUET
Michel Corrette
(1712-1768)
Allegretto
117
mf

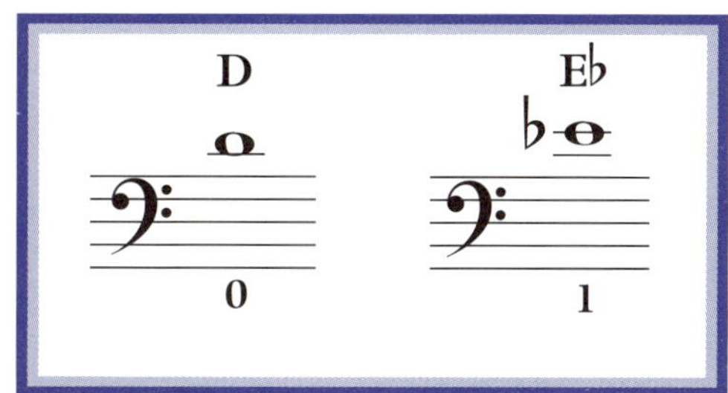

TWO WAYS - SAME SOUND

118
119

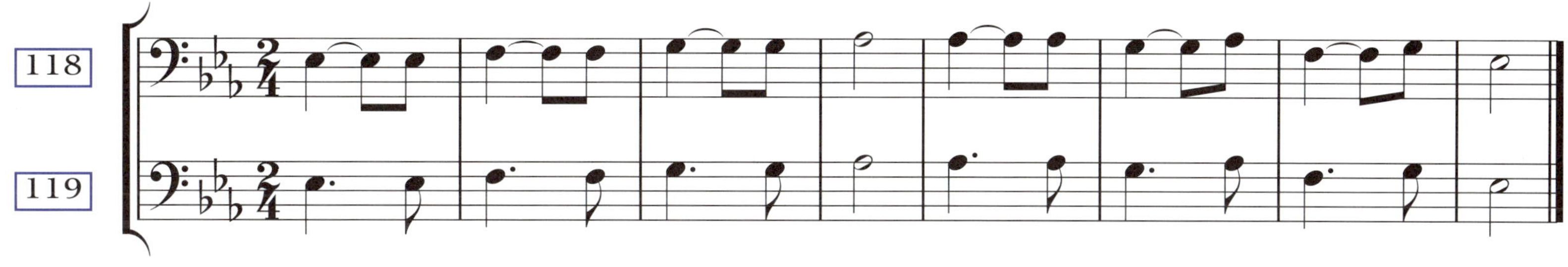

ALMA MATER

Andante

College Song

120

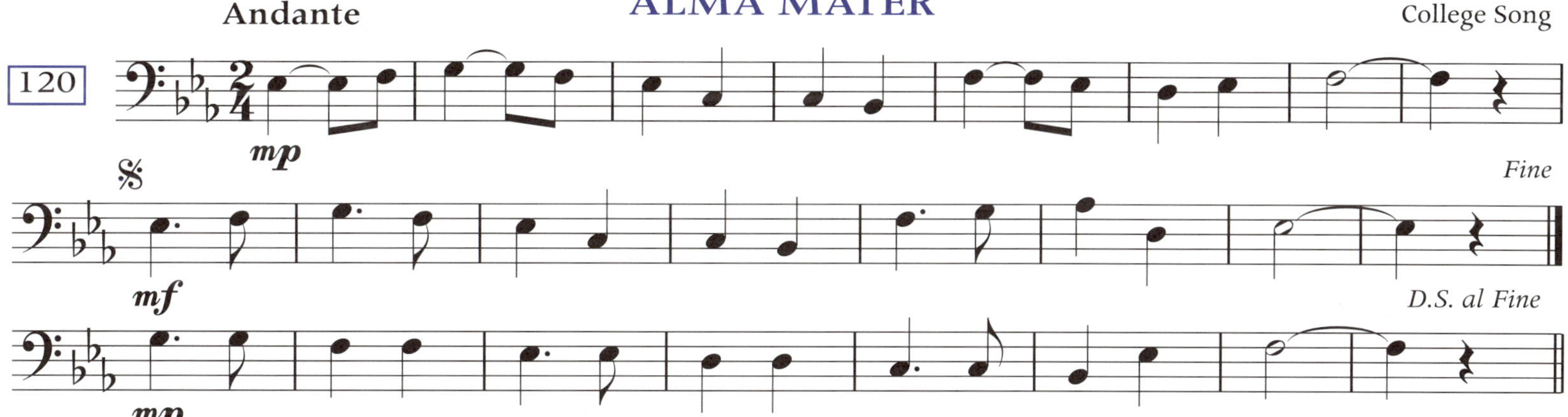

OLD BRASS WAGON

Moderato

American Pioneer Song

121

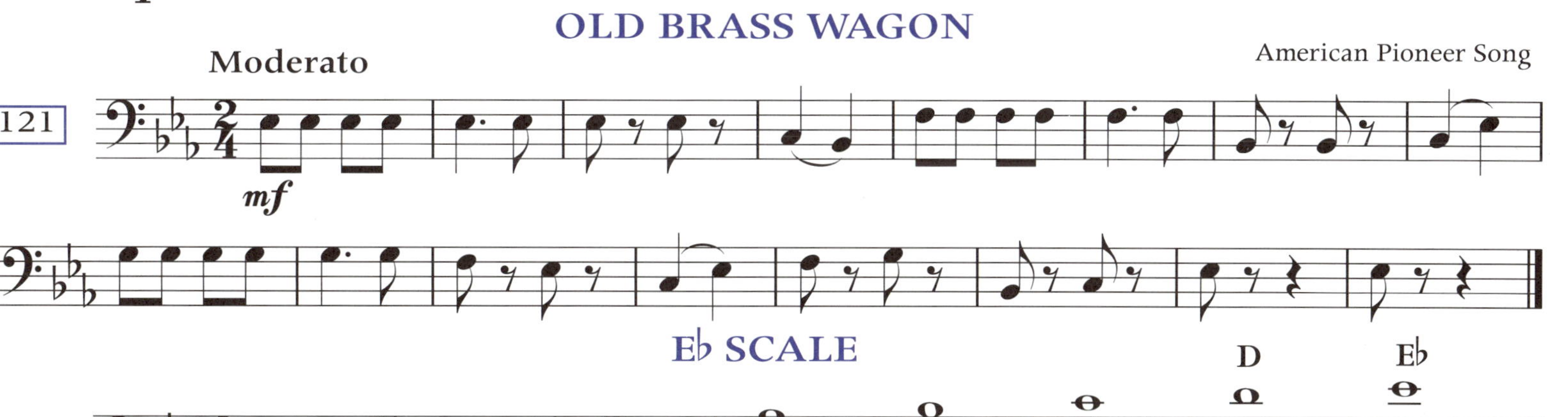

E♭ SCALE

122

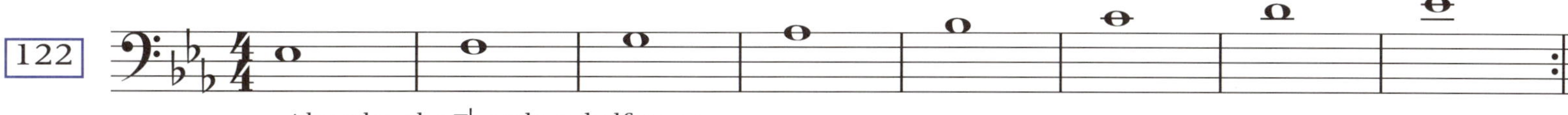

Also play the E♭ scale as half notes.

KUM BA YAH

Andante

Spiritual

123

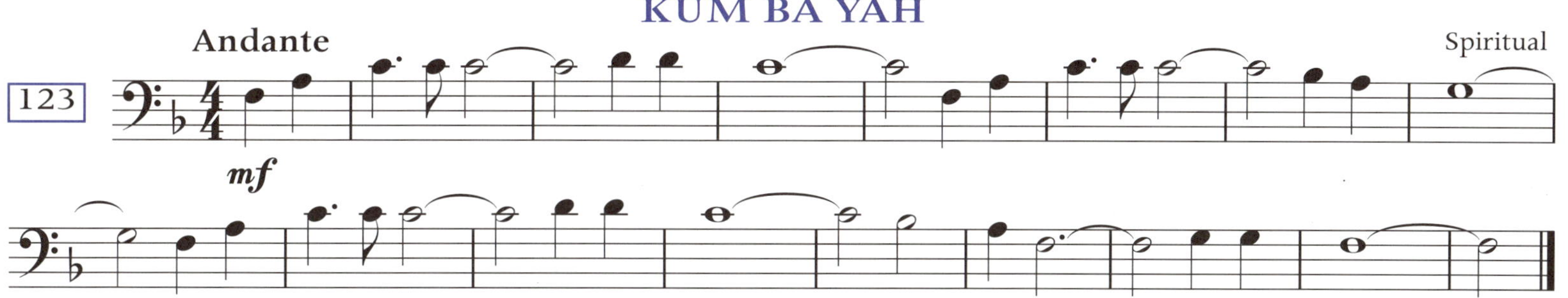

Play Premier Rhythm Lines 19 and 20 on page 43.

Play Premier Technique Lines 19 and 20 on page 45.

TEMPO

MAESTOSO

Stately

TENUTO

—

Hold the note for its full value.

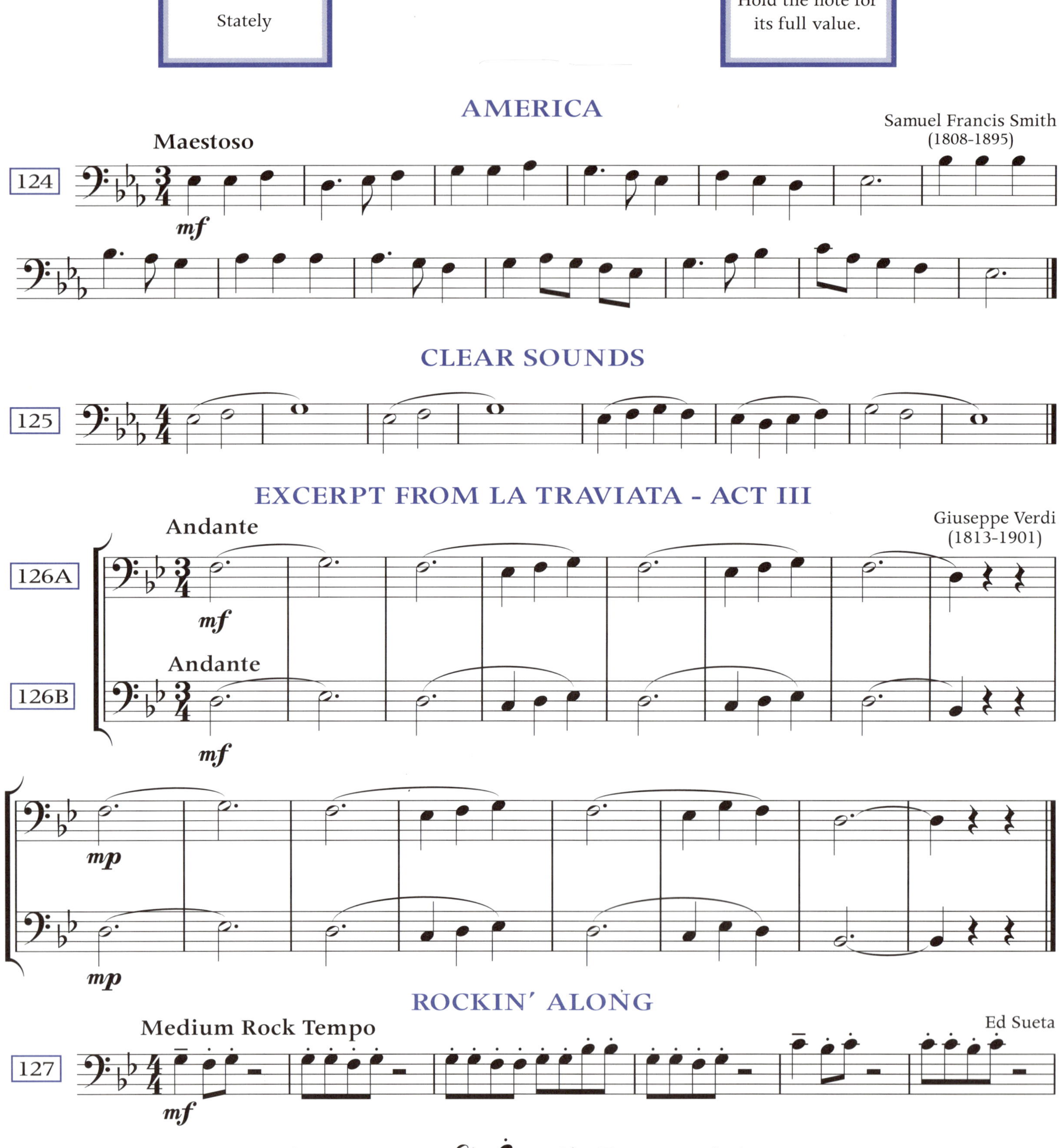

COMMODORE MARCH

Quincy Hilliard

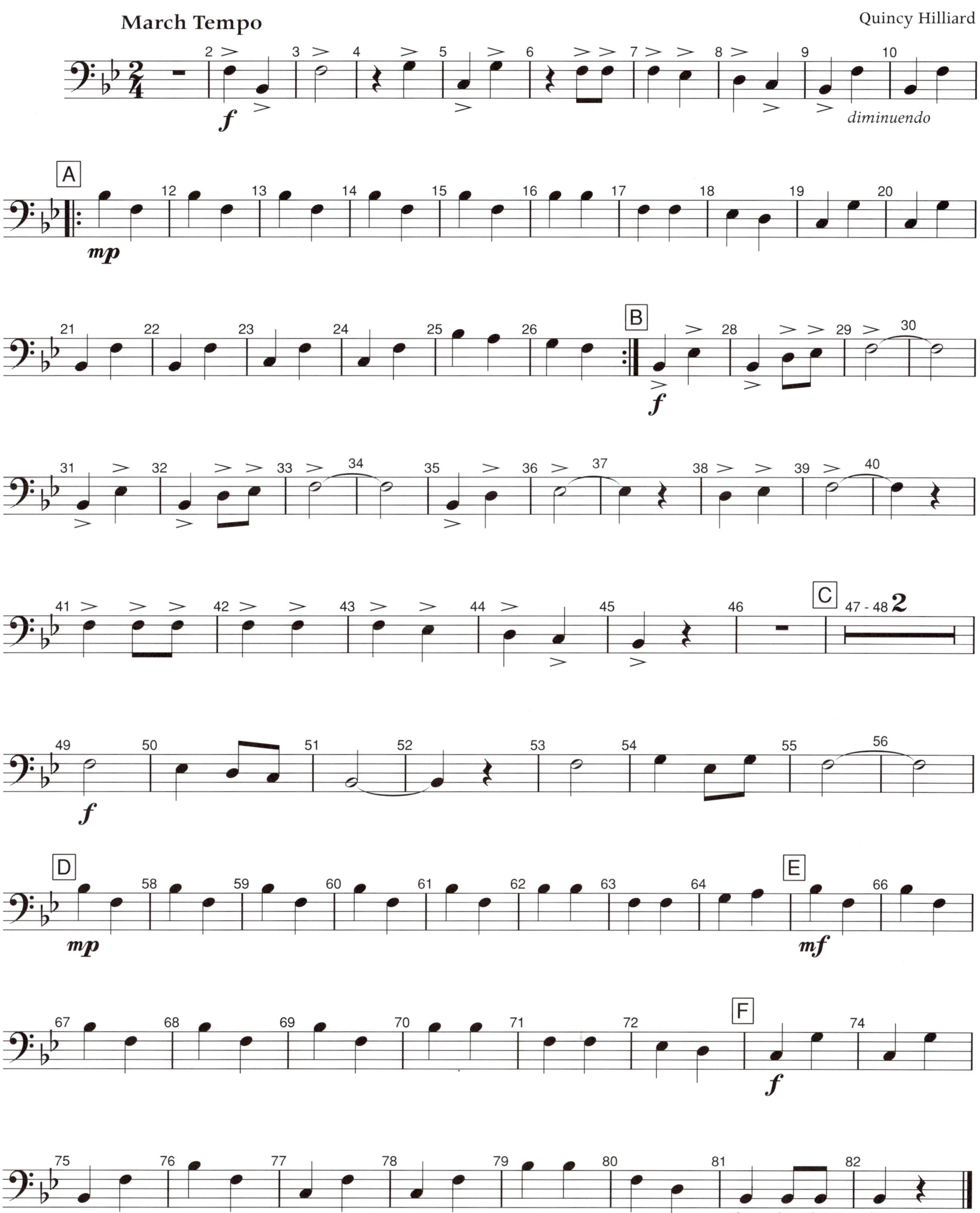

MARCH

George Frederich Handel
(1685-1759)

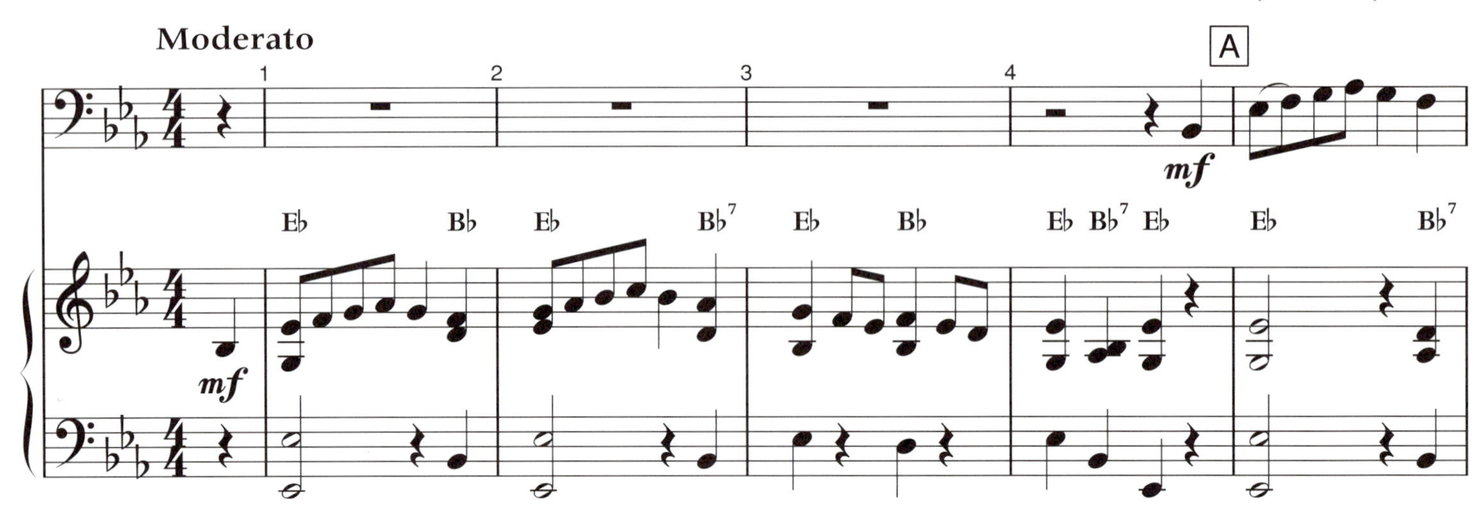

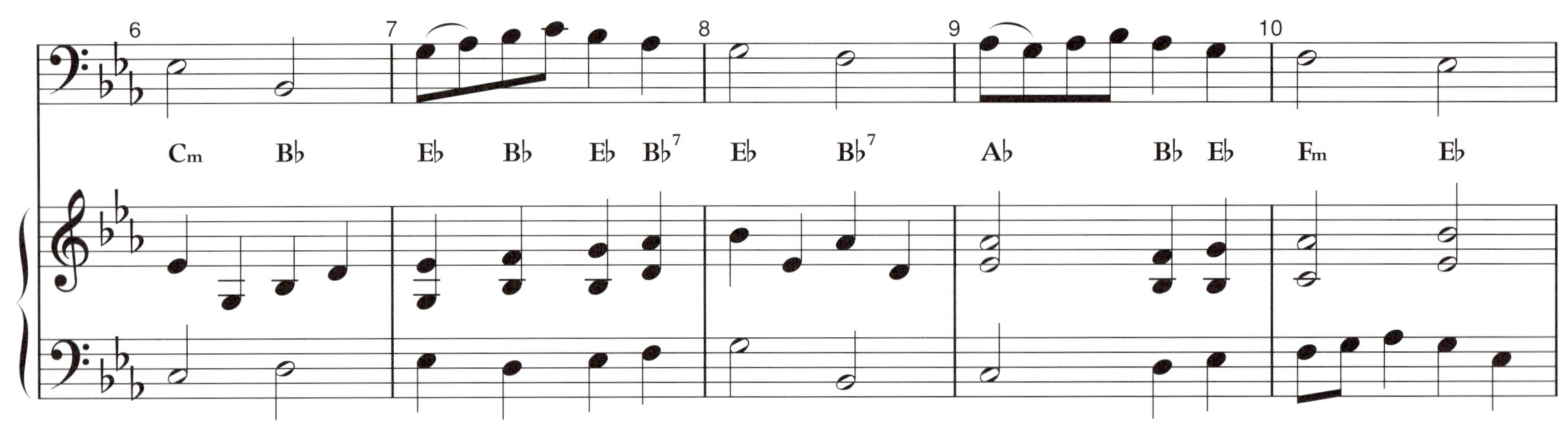

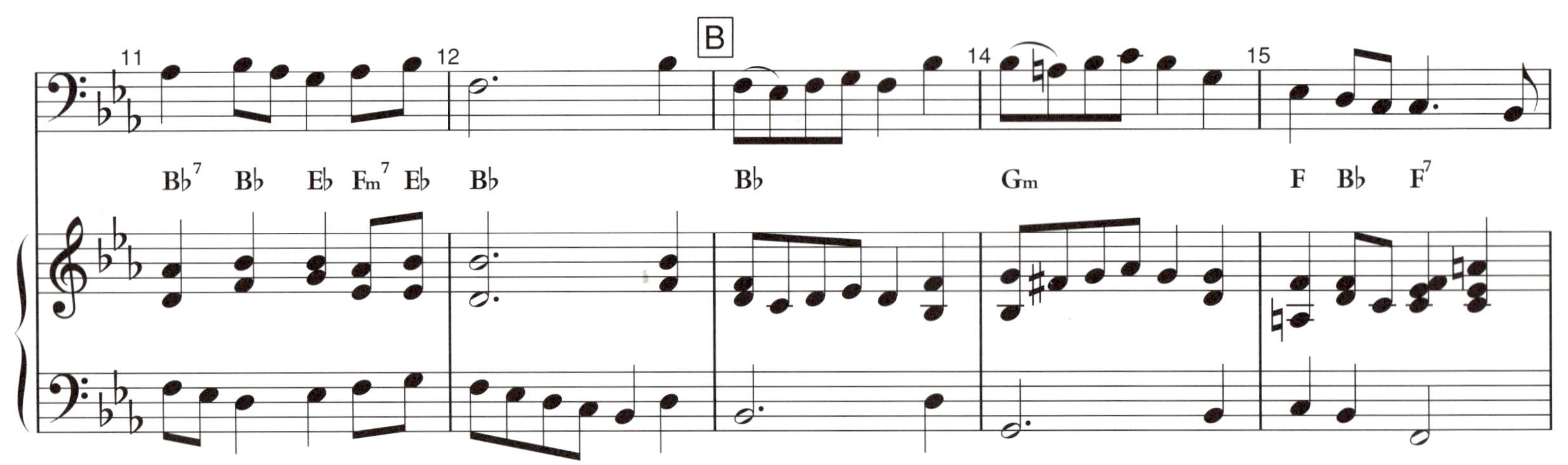

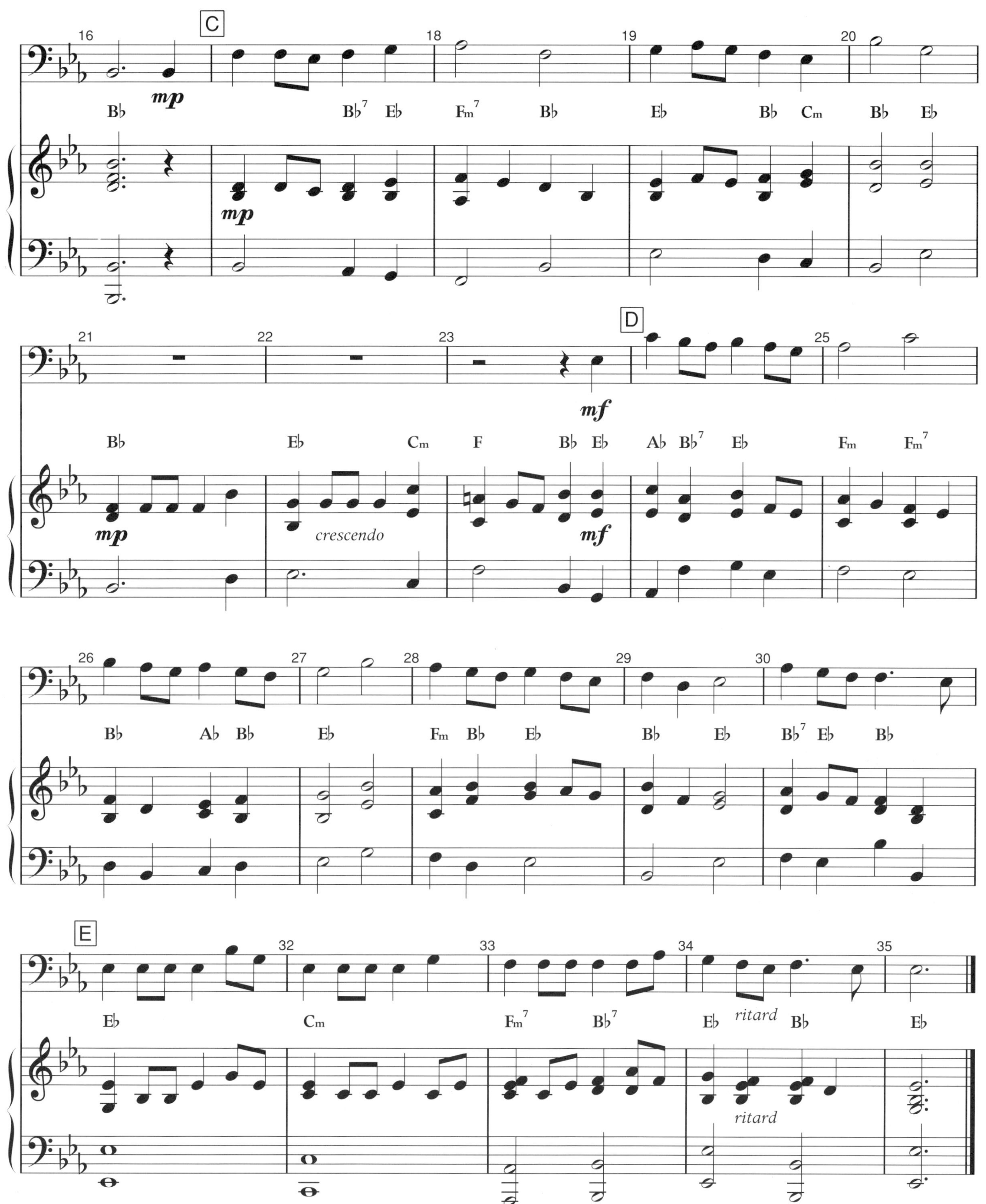
C
16
18
19
20
mp
B♭
B♭7
E♭
Fm7
B♭
E♭
B♭
Cm
B♭
E♭
mp
D
21
22
23
25
mf
B♭
E♭
Cm
F
B♭
E♭
A♭
B♭7
E♭
Fm
Fm7
mp
crescendo
mf
26
27
28
29
30
B♭
A♭
B♭
E♭
Fm
B♭
E♭
B♭
E♭
B♭7
E♭
B♭
E
32
33
34
35
E♭
Cm
Fm7
B♭7
E♭
ritard
B♭
E♭
ritard

ALPINE OVERTURE

Quincy Hilliard

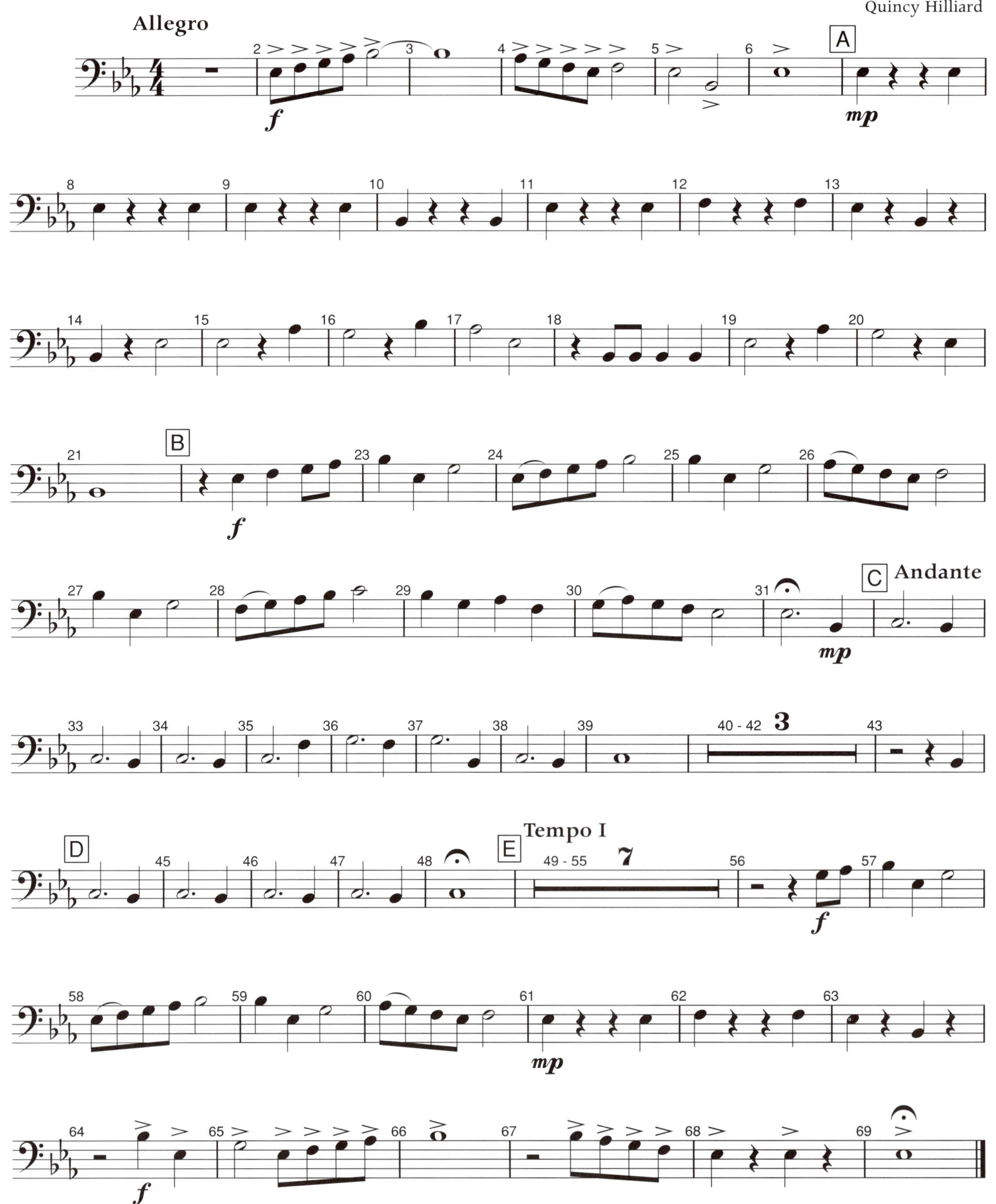

MAJOR SCALES AND ARPEGGIOS

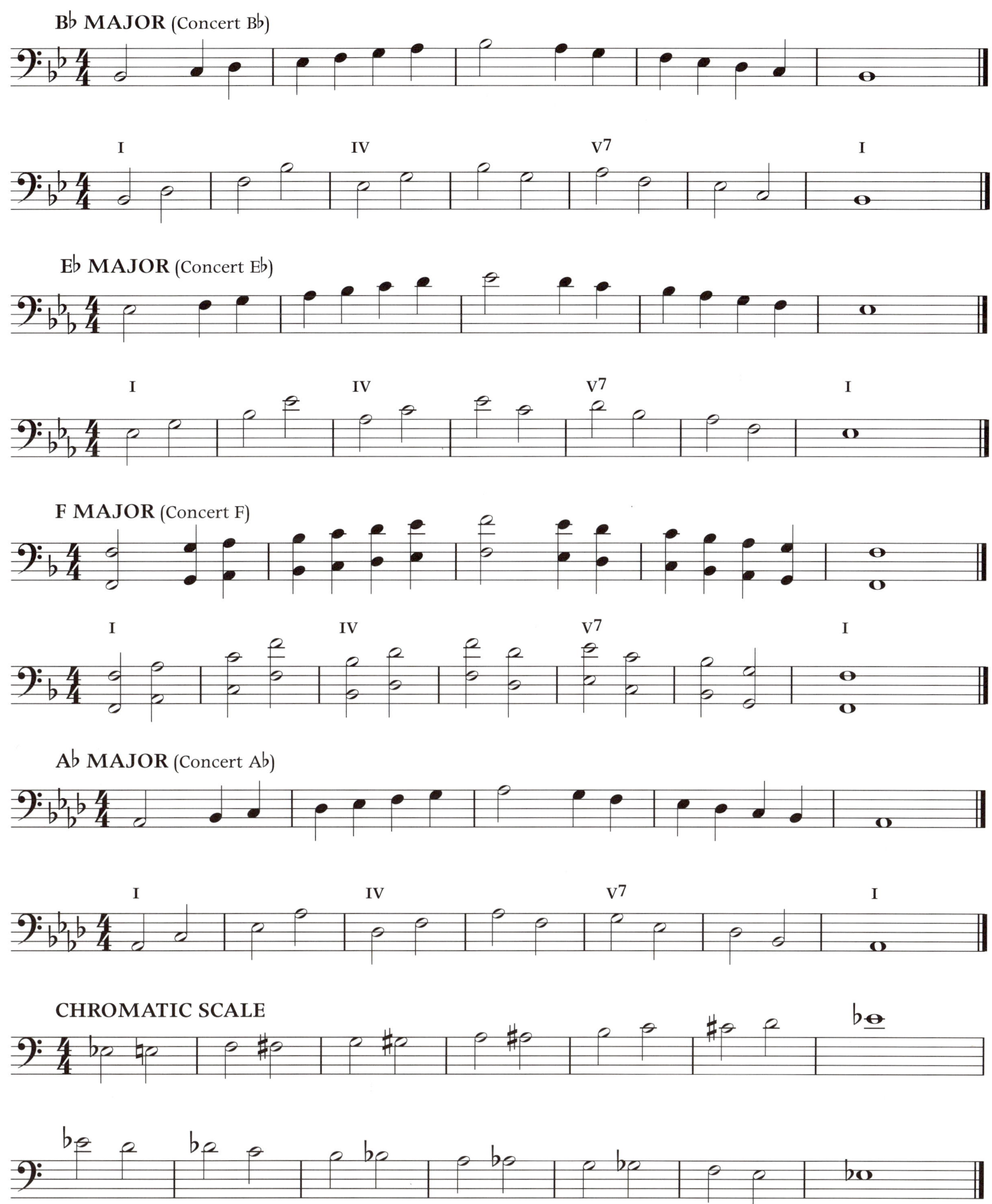

PREMIER RHYTHMS

1. Clap and **SAY** each line.
2. Clap and **THINK** each line.
3. **PLAY** each line on any of the notes you have learned.
4. After a line becomes easy, **INCREASE** your speed.

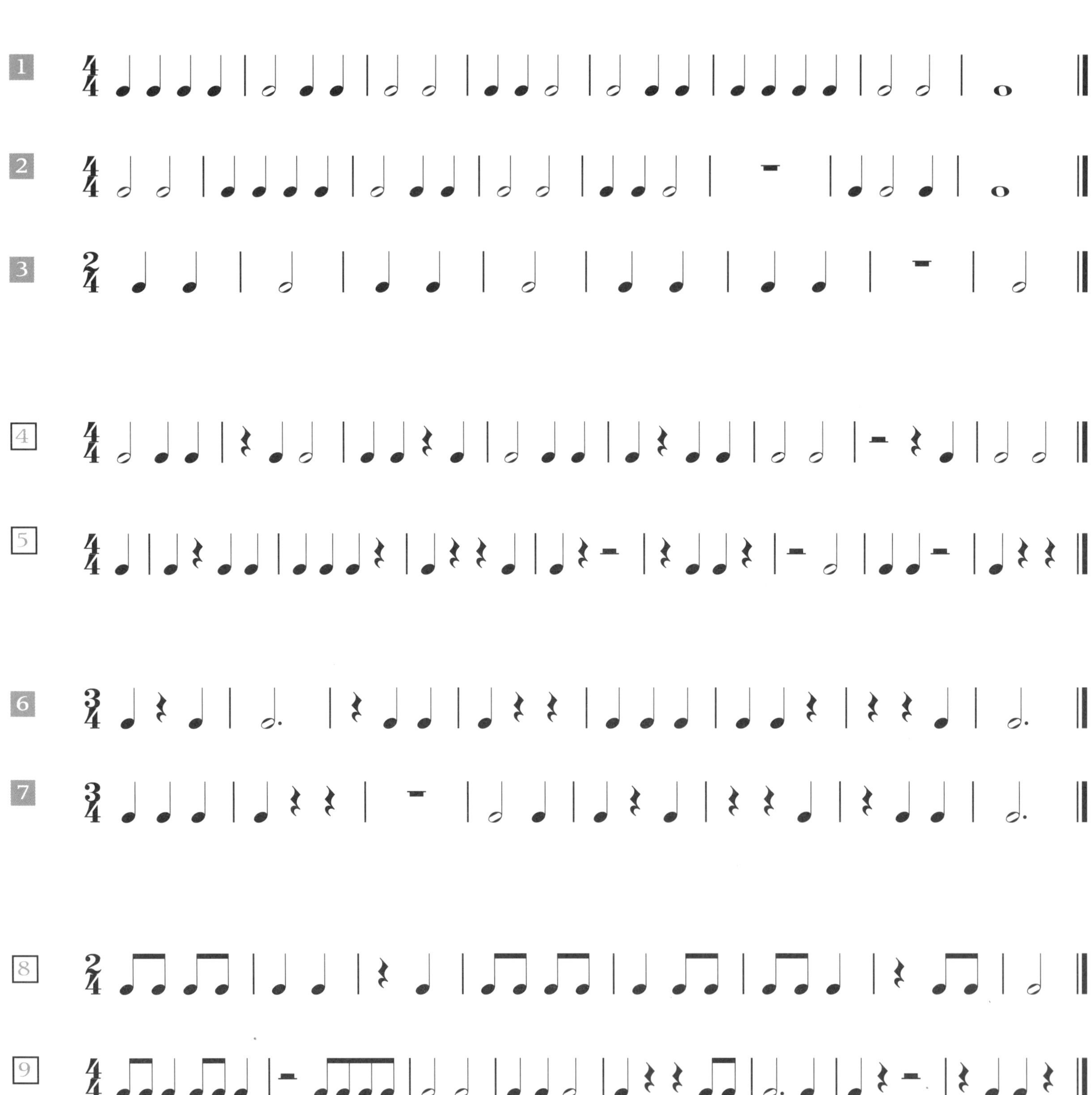

11 2/4

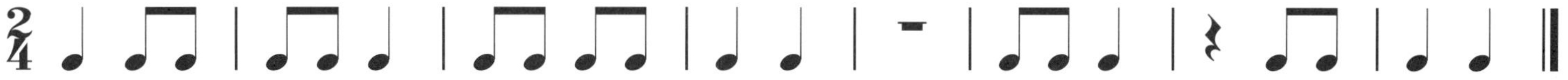

12 3/4

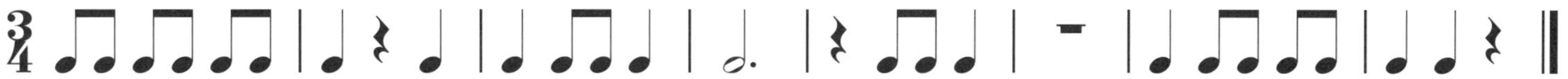

13 2/4

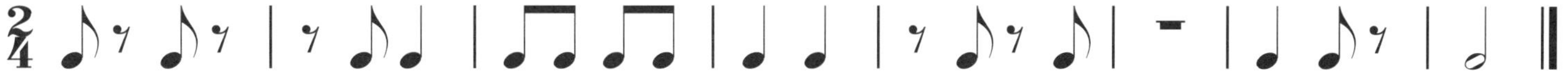

14 4/4

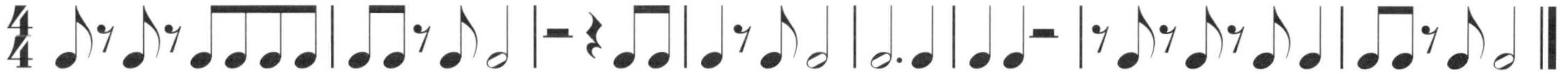

15 4/4

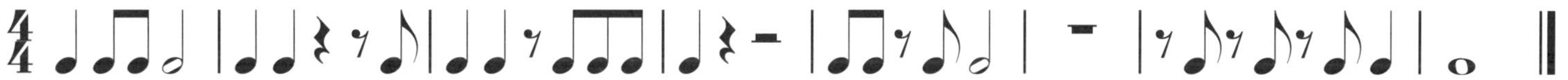

16 3/4

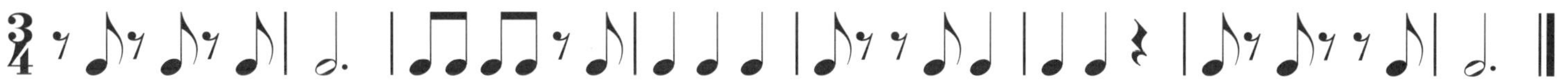

17 4/4

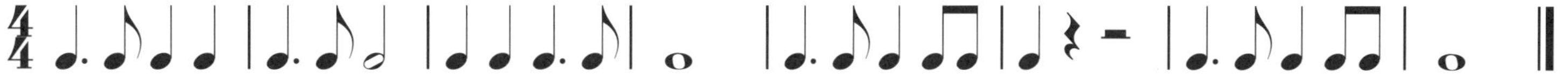

18 4/4

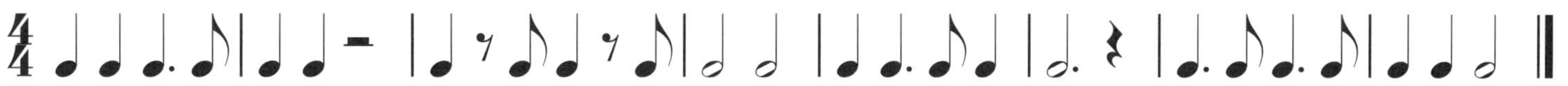

19 2/4

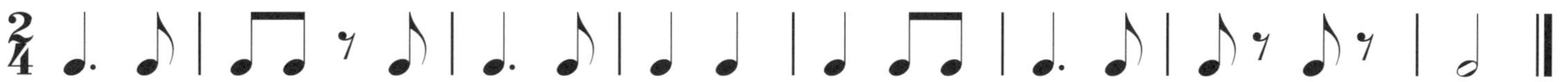

20 3/4

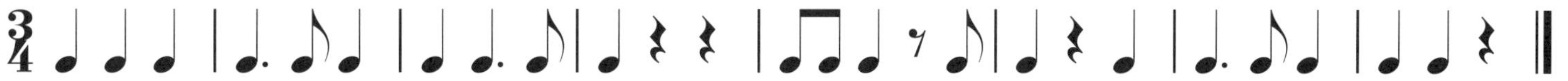

PREMIER TECHNIQUE

1. **PLAY** each line several times.
2. Always be **ACCURATE**.
3. Always keep your fingers **CLOSE** to the tops of the valves.
4. When a line becomes easy, **INCREASE** your speed.

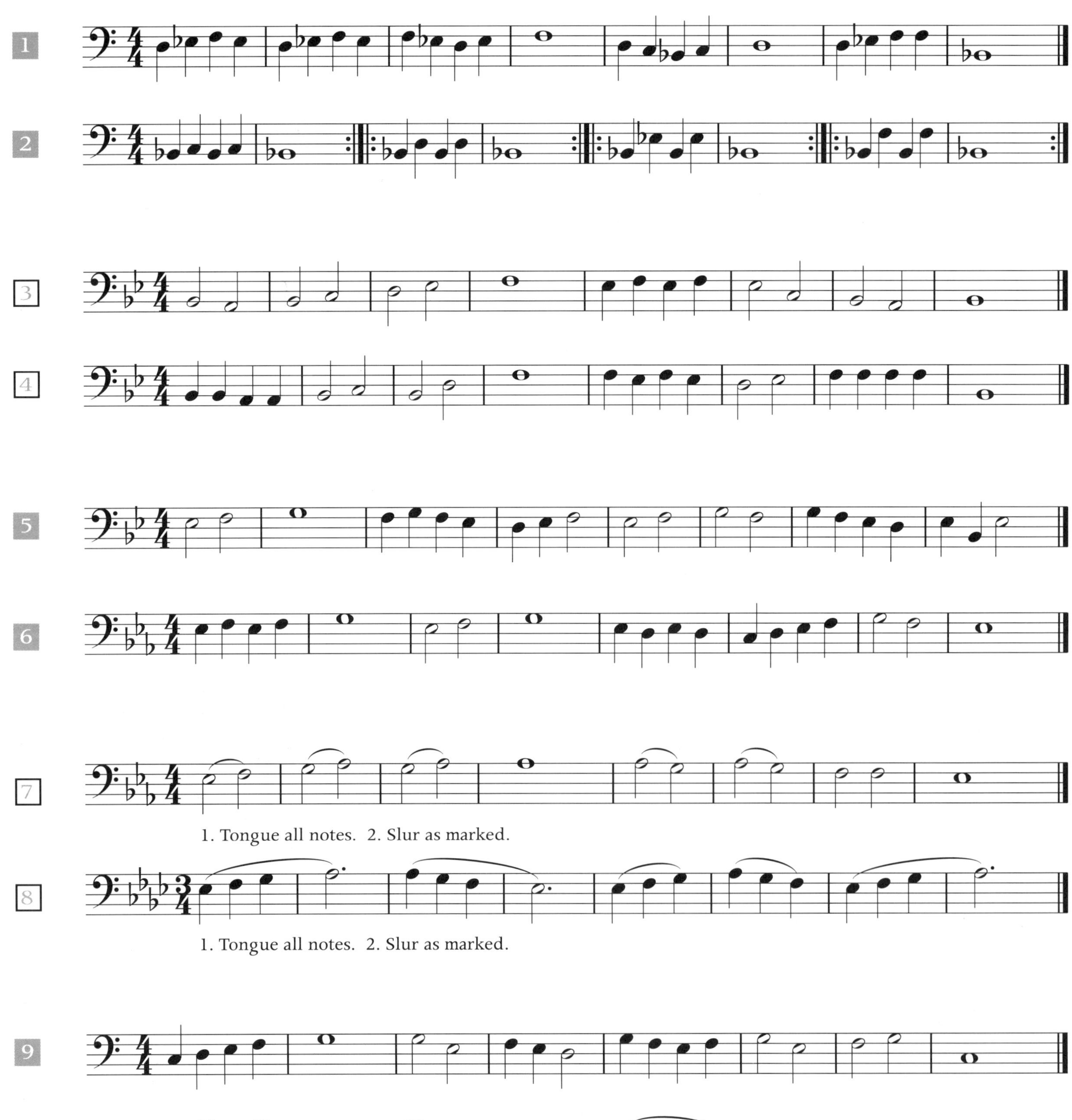

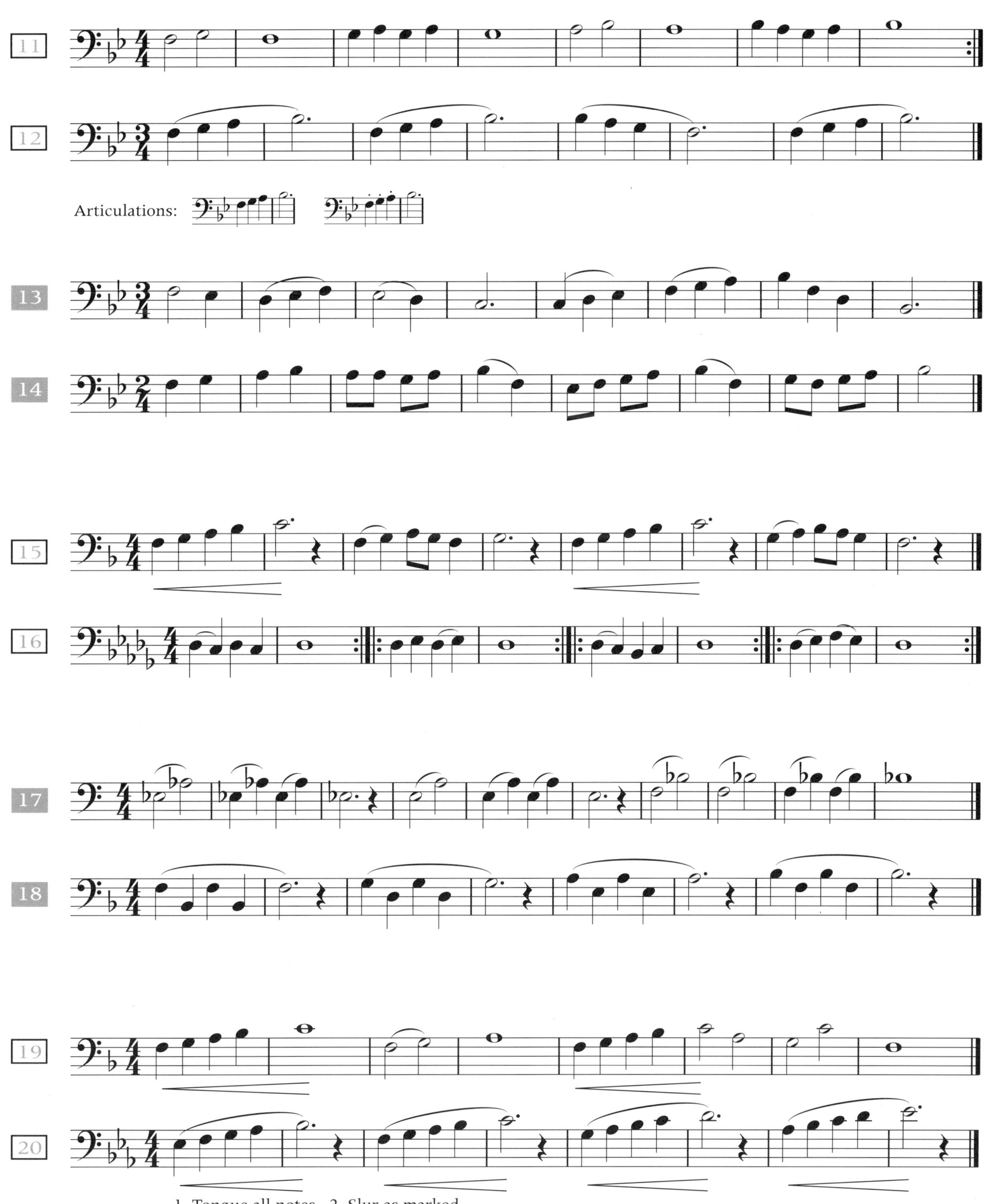

1. Tongue all notes. 2. Slur as marked.

THE HISTORY OF THE BARITONE AND EUPHONIUM

The baritone horn is a valved, brass instrument. It is considered the tenor instrument of the tuba family and has the same pitch as the trombone. Today, most baritones are made of brass and are usually lacquered or plated with silver or nickel.

The baritone first appeared in Germany in 1830 and was generally referred to as the "baritonhorn." The euphonium, a type of baritone, has a wider bell which results in a mellower tone. While the baritone has three valves, the euphonium may have four or even five valves.

The euphonium was invented in 1843 by Sommer of Weimar and was widely used by Russian and German brass and military bands. Today, it is used mostly in the United States. Notable composers who have written special parts for the euphonium in their music include Strauss, Stravinsky and Holst.

By the middle of the 1800s, instrument makers were producing many different baritones with minor differences in the size of the bore and the flare of the bell. Today, baritones are still made in different sizes and styles.

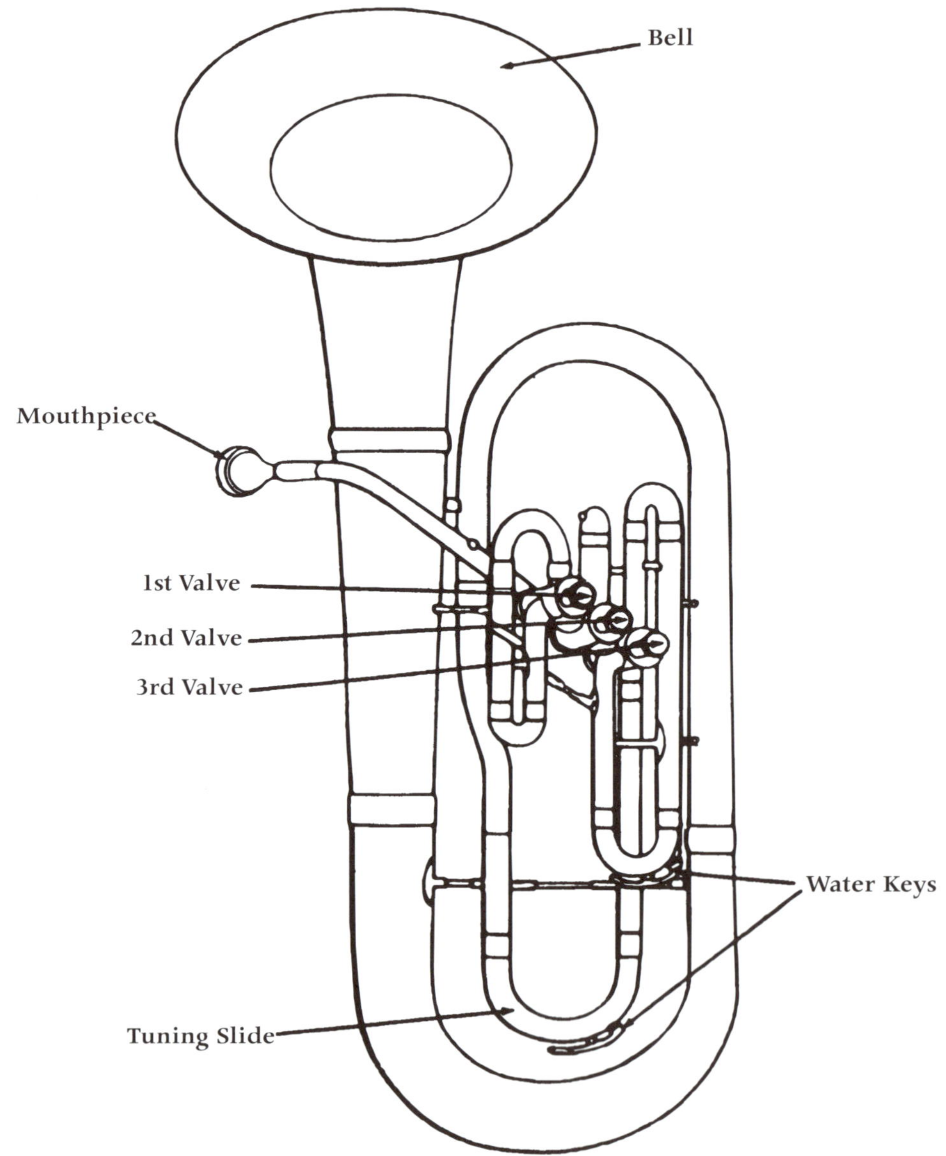

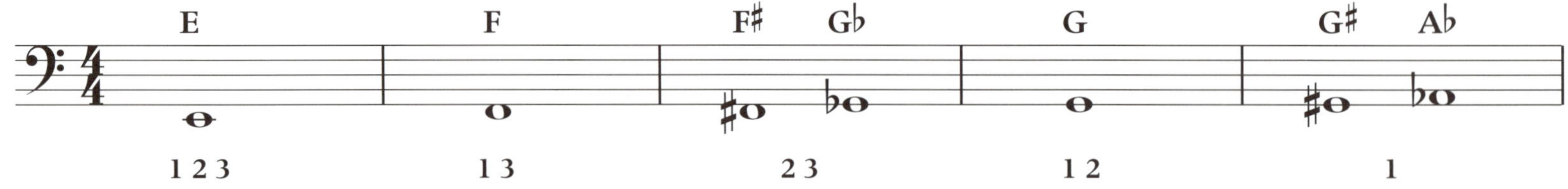

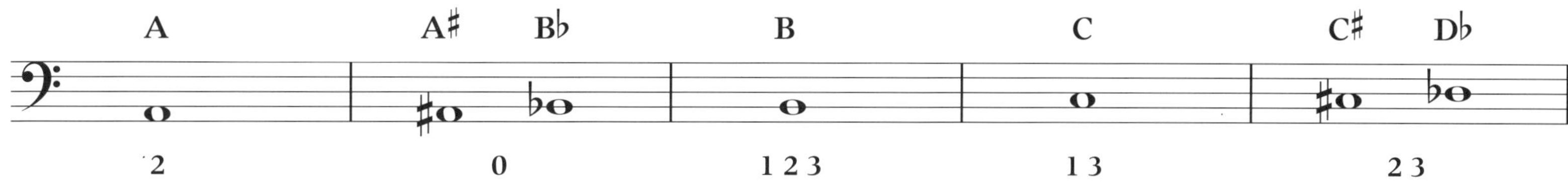

D
D♯ E♭
E
F
F♯ G♭
1 2
1
2
0
2 3

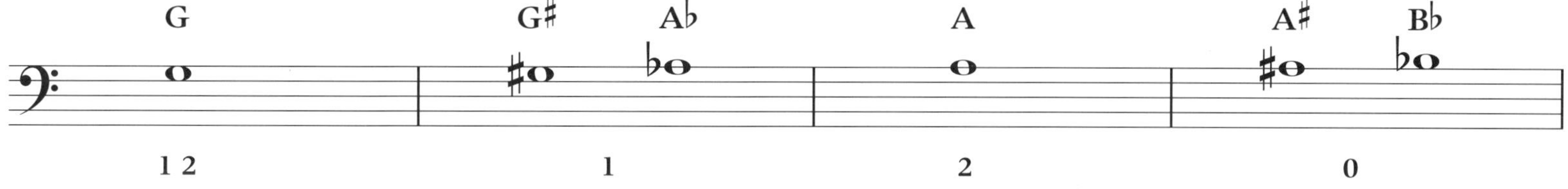

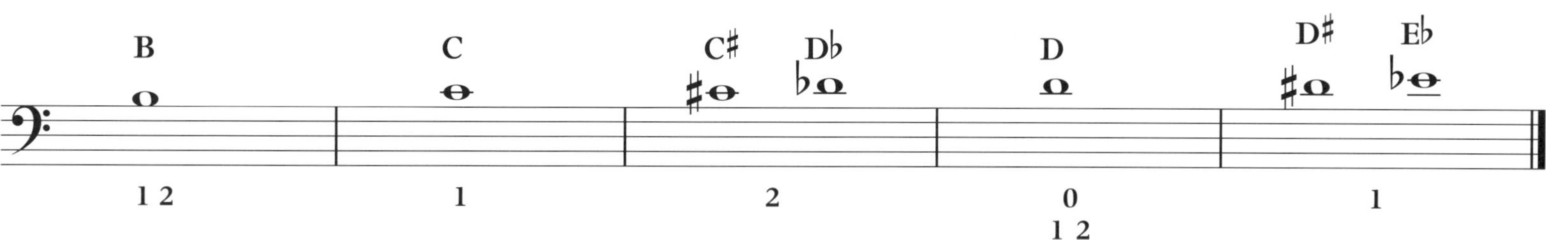

MUSIC DICTIONARY

MUSICAL SYMBOLS

Symbol	Term	Definition
	Accent	Emphasis is given to a note by playing it a little louder
	Accidental	A sharp (♯), flat (♭), or natural (♮) not indicated in the key signature
	Breath Mark	A place to take a breath
	Coda	Ending section of a composition
C	Common Time	Same as 4/4 time
	Crescendo	Gradually louder
	Diminuendo	Gradually softer
V	Dominant Chord	A chord built on the fifth note of the scale
	Fermata	Hold the note or rest a little longer
♭	Flat	Lowers the pitch of a note one half step
♮	Natural	Cancels a sharp or flat until the next bar line
	One measure repeat	Repeat the previous measure
2	Two measure repeat	Repeat the previous two measures
	Repeat Sign	Play the music again from the beginning
♯	Sharp	Raises the pitch of a note one half step
	Slur	A curved line that connects notes of different pitches
	Staccato	Separated; detached
IV	Subdominant Chord	A chord built on the fourth note of the scale
	Tenuto	Hold the note for its full value
	Tie	A curved line that connects notes of the same pitch
I	Tonic Chord	A chord built on the first note of the scale

MUSICAL TERMS

Accelerando (Accel.)	Gradually faster
A Tempo	Resume the original speed
Cantabile	Singing style
Da Capo al Fine	Go back to the beginning and play to the *Fine*
Dal Segno al Coda	Go back to the sign (𝄋) and play to the *Coda*
Dal Segno al Fine	Go back to the sign (𝄋) and play to the *Fine*
Divisi	Some players play the upper notes while other players play the lower notes
Duet	A composition with parts for two players
Espressivo	With expression
Excerpt	A part of a composition
Key Signature	The sharp(s) or flat(s) placed to the right of a clef on a staff which indicate(s) which notes are to be sharped or flatted
Legato	Smoothly; play smoothly with no separation between the notes
Phrase	A musical sentence
Pick-up note(s)	Note(s) before the first complete measure of a song
Rallentando (Rall.)	Gradually slower
Ritardando (Rit.)	Gradually slower
Round	Playing the same music but beginning at different times
Simile	The same; continue in the same manner
Solo	One person plays
Tacet	Silent
Theme	The main melody in a musical composition
Unison	All players play the same pitch

DYNAMICS (Loud and Soft) MARKINGS

pp	*pianissimo*	Very soft
p	*piano*	Soft
mp	*mezzo piano*	Moderately soft
mf	*mezzo forte*	Moderately loud
f	*forte*	Loud
ff	*fortissimo*	Very loud

TEMPO (Speed) MARKINGS

Adagio	Slow
Allegretto	Moderately fast
Allegro	Fast and lively
Andante	Moderately slow
Con Spirito	With spirit
Largo	Very slow; flowing
Maestoso	Majestically; stately
Moderato	Moderate speed
Presto	Very fast; faster than allegro
Vivace	Lively; briskly